# *By the Grace of God*

JOHN FOGG

The opinions expressed in this manuscript are solely the opinions of the author and do not represent the opinions or thoughts of the publisher. The author has represented and warranted full ownership and/or legal right to publish all the materials in this book.

By the Grace of God
All Rights Reserved.
Copyright © 2014 John Fogg
v3.0

Cover Photo © 2014 John Fogg. All rights reserved - used with permission.

This book may not be reproduced, transmitted, or stored in whole or in part by any means, including graphic, electronic, or mechanical without the express written consent of the publisher except in the case of brief quotations embodied in critical articles and reviews.

Outskirts Press, Inc.
http://www.outskirtspress.com

Paperback ISBN: 978-1-4787-1314-2
Hardback ISBN: 978-1-4787-2515-2

Outskirts Press and the "OP" logo are trademarks belonging to Outskirts Press, Inc.

PRINTED IN THE UNITED STATES OF AMERICA

# Contents

Acknowledgements .................................................................. v
Author's Preface................................................................... vii
Chapter 1: Setting the Stage ...............................................1
Chapter 2: The El Centro Mishap ......................................5
Chapter 3: The Lakehurst Mishap....................................17
Chapter 4: The Blue Angels in Transition .....................23
Chapter 5: Out of the Blue................................................27
Chapter 6: Hurricane Frederic .........................................35
Chapter 7: Intuition ...........................................................51
Chapter 8: Coincidence.....................................................57
Chapter 9: The 11:11 Phenomenon ................................59
Chapter 10: Drawn to the Bible ......................................61
Chapter 11: The Viet Nam Experience...........................67
Chapter 12: The Gear Up Landing .................................73
Chapter 13: The Ruptured Natural Gas Line................77
Chapter 14: Divine Intervention .....................................79
Chapter 15: How Did This Happen? ..............................83
Chapter 16: The Awakening.............................................89
About the Author ................................................................95

# Acknowledgements

My wife Pat and I have been talking about this book for several years and I would write bits and pieces of each of the stories but never gained the momentum to finish the book. There were always distractions related to employment and other commitments. But in the last year, time was more available and with Pat's strong support and encouragement, this book is now a completed work. My thanks to The Reverend Eric Long, Richard McCool, Allison Sanchez and my mother-in-law, Joyce Massey, for their support and input.

This book is dedicated to Pat, my wife of 39 years. Without her enthusiastic and unwavering belief in me and the importance of this book, *By the Grace of God* might not have become a reality.

# Author's Preface

This book's title really captures what I want to communicate to my readers. It is *By the Grace of God* that I am here today to tell the stories contained in this book. You will read of combat air missions in Viet Nam, you will live through a fight for your life during a category four hurricane on a 36 foot sailboat, you will feel the excitement of being in the cockpit of a Blue Angel jet and vicariously experience a spiritual awakening that changed my life forever. If you consider yourself to be a Christian, I hope this book will strengthen your faith and your relationship with God. If you don't have a strong faith in God as described in the New Testament of the Bible, I hope the events described in this book will help open your mind and heart to the possibility of having a personal relationship with God that will change your life forever.

CHAPTER 1

# Setting the Stage

IN THE FALL of 1994, some extraordinary events began to unfold in my life for which there could be no rational explanation. I didn't realize it then, but my life would change forever for the better. What happened to me is available to all of us if we will just open our minds and our hearts to the possibility of miracles. As I look back on those experiences, it can best be described as the emergence of a spiritual reality in my material world. As it was happening, I had no clue as to its origin or purpose. I was not seeking some spiritual awareness or awakening, quite the opposite, I was the Mayor of Pensacola, Florida and I thought my life was filled with purpose and opportunity by my standards at the time. After serving as a fighter pilot in the U.S. Marine Corps for twenty years, I retired as a Lieutenant Colonel in Pensacola, Florida, the birthplace of Naval Aviation. My wife Pat is a Pensacola native and we both knew we would retire from the Marine Corps and begin the next chapter of our lives here. When you serve on active duty in America's military, it is not unusual to relocate every two or three years so it is difficult to put down roots and establish strong and lasting relationships with people, something Pat and I desired and looked forward to. So in April of 1987, we relocated to Pensacola to begin the transition to civilian life. Before relating those early retirement experiences, it is important to understand the context of my military background as it relates to the spiritual awakening mentioned above.

God blessed me with the skill sets required to fly tactical jet fighters and from early childhood, I knew I wanted to be a pilot. I spent a good part of my childhood building model airplanes and flying "U" control gas powered planes. Fast forward to college graduation, commissioning and assignment to active duty in the summer of 1967. In the course of a twenty year career with the Marine Corps, I flew 200 combat air missions in Viet Nam and for two years, was assigned to and flew off the USS Forrestal. I was selected to fly as the Marine Corps Representative with the Blue Angels (left wing and slot pilot), graduated from the Navy Fighter Weapons School, "Top Gun" and served as the Commanding Officer of VMFA 122, a Marine Corps fighter squadron based in Beaufort, SC. There are many other details of my Marine Corps experience that are important to this spiritual discussion and I will relate some of them later in this book. For now, it is fair to say I was blessed to have the best assignments you could hope for if you are a U.S. Marine Corps fighter pilot. Flying was my passion. Every time I strapped into the cockpit of a jet aircraft, it was as if the airplane became an extension of my body. I always felt the jet and I became one being. With that as background, let's talk about my experiences in Pensacola after retirement from the Corps.

## SETTING THE STAGE

As soon as we relocated to Pensacola, I pursued opportunities to get involved in the community in any way I could. A friend of the family encouraged the leadership of the Naval Aviation Museum Foundation to interview me for the position of National Capital Campaign Director for the Phase III expansion of the National Museum of Naval Aviation. I jumped at the opportunity to be part of one of the premier organizations in our community and helped fund the construction of what has become the number one museum attraction in the southeast. Further, the Pensacola Area Chamber of Commerce was about to go through the reaccreditation process so I volunteered to help which allowed me get to know many of the business leaders in the area. At the same time, the City of Pensacola was conducting an airport master plan update and Federal Aviation Regulation(FAR) part 150 noise study and I was asked to chair the committee. The political arena has always been an interest of mine so when the City Councilman in my District decided to vacate his District seat and run At-Large, Pat and I talked it over and we decided I should run for the District 3 seat on the council. We conducted a vigorous door to door campaign which, for me, was one of the most gratifying aspects of running for elected office. There were three other candidates in the race for District 3 and we won the seat without a runoff. I was re-elected to the District 3 seat for two more two year terms and on July 29, 1994, I was appointed Mayor of the City of Pensacola and served in that position for over fourteen years. In 2001, I became the first elected Mayor since 1913. It was shortly after being appointed Mayor that a series of events began to unfold that would change my life and my view of the world forever.

## ⊰ BY THE GRACE OF GOD

I was not a particularly religious person but I did consider myself to be a Christian, and the events I am about to describe in this book served to strengthen my belief in God and in Jesus Christ as described in the New Testament. In the course of my life, there have been many events or circumstances that could have easily resulted in my death. At the time, I attributed my survival to my ability to skillfully pilot an airplane or luck or a combination of both. Now I know that God has been at work in my life (and yours) since the beginning, even though I was not aware of it. There are several subjects that will be addressed in this book and they include the importance of intuition; the power contained in each moment we live; awareness of what some call synchronicities or coincidences; the depth of God's love for us and the need for us to seek God's will in our lives. My purpose in writing this book is to share my experiences with the spiritual world in the hope that your faith in God through Jesus Christ and the Holy Spirit will be made stronger and that those of you who have not experienced a personal relationship with God will open your mind and heart to that possibility. Let's begin with some experiences as a tactical jet fighter pilot flying as the Marine Corps representative with the Blue Angels that had a major role in setting the stage. Since the inception of the Blue Angels in 1946, their safety record has been extraordinarily good, especially considering they are in the airshow business. Nineteen seventy-three, however, would prove to be an exception.

CHAPTER 2

# The El Centro Mishap

*Photo by Ron Rentfrow*     *Captain John Fogg 1973*

I WAS SELECTED to fly with the Blues in late 1972 for the 1973 and 1974 airshow seasons. The Team was flying the McDonnell Douglas F-4 Phantom in those days and the F-4

## BY THE GRACE OF GOD

was the aircraft I flew in the fleet. The F-4 was the largest tactical jet fighter the Blues ever flew, capable of MACH 2 plus (twice the speed of sound) and it measured over 60 feet long with two J-79 jet engines with afterburners producing over 36,000 pounds of thrust. We used to joke that the F-4 was proof that, with enough thrust, a brick can fly. The Blues fly six jets in every airshow with four in the diamond, echelon, line abreast and trail formations and two solo pilots demonstrating the high performance capabilities of the Phantom. Three of the six pilots are new each year and the second year guys train the new pilots.

In my first orientation with the Team, the second year pilots told the new guys what the standards would be for the flight demonstration. The goal of the Blues is to fly the most difficult maneuvers that can be flown safely, to fly those maneuvers closer than any other team in the world which was defined as 36 inches wingtip to canopy and to fly the maneuvers with no visible movement from the ground. I got a kick out of one of the second year guys when he said "you can move around (in formation) all you want, plus or minus six inches." Please understand that plus or minus six inches is a standard that is unimaginable when flying a jet aircraft weighing almost 60,000 pounds at over 450 nautical miles (KTS) per hour. The Blue Angels depart for winter training at Naval Air Facility (NAF) El Centro, California in early January every year and return to NAS Pensacola in March to begin the airshow circuit.

## THE EL CENTRO MISHAP

In the early 1970's, we scheduled two flights a day with no planned days off for the ten weeks of scheduled training. To prevent any distractions, family members were not allowed to visit the team while they are in winter training. The first brief started at an hour and a half before sunrise and first launch would be at sunrise. After the flight, we would debrief and then brief for the second flight. The debriefs can really be brutal. Each of the demonstration pilot's lives are totally dependent on everyone doing their job right and each member has to be totally honest about everyone's performance. Further, the goal is perfection in each of the maneuvers and that almost never happens so you have to check your ego at the door and be willing to listen and learn. We would finish the flight training by about 2:00 PM and then do some sort of physical training for a couple of hours. For me, that meant some intense games of racket ball. The training flights of 1973 were going well. We were briefing for the next to last training flight before beginning the airshow season and we were all excited to finish the training process and looked forward to joining the airshow circuit. We started the brief before sunrise and we manned our jets just after sun-up. Almost every take-off is done in diamond formation so when we were cleared for take-off we would take the runway in what is called a finger four formation. The typical Navy/Marine Corps runway is 150 feet wide and the F-4 was so big our formation would consume the entire width of the runway. In order to perform the take-off, we would have to completely overlap the wings of the jets even to the extent the outboard wing panels would overlap the intakes of the wingmen. The Boss would add power to 100%, release the brakes and call for afterburner. The Boss would get airborne first and the wingmen would stay on the ground until the Boss's wingtips were above the wingmen's canopies. As soon as #2 and #3 were airborne sufficiently, #4 or the slot pilot would make the move into the slot position and with all four jets in the diamond formation, the Boss would lead us into a maximum performance climb. Every time we performed that maneuver, I remember thinking about the emergency procedures in the event we had to abort the take-off. With all the overlap we had, it was a complicated process of reduction of power, chute deployment and braking in a specific order. Thank God we never had to execute that procedure. When I first joined the Team, I remember vividly being in total disbelief when the Boss and slot pilot put me in the back seat of the slot's jet and took me on an orientation flight. The distance from the Boss's jet to the wingman's jet was unbelievably close. Actually, it was very uncomfortable.

Anyway, we proceeded to the restricted area and began the airshow sequence. We had completed a little more than half the airshow practice and we set up for the trail loop. In this maneuver, the three wingmen are stacked down and aft of the lead jet. It's a difficult maneuver because you can only see the jet immediately above you and the look-up angle is acute. The Trail Loop is supposed to go like this. From behind the crowd, the Boss would call "Coming left for the trail loop" and the slot pilot would call the diamond to "Go trail." We (the wingmen) would adjust our positions anticipating the left turn and subsequent rollout aligning the formation with the runway. The Boss would call "Rolling out" followed by

## THE EL CENTRO MISHAP

"Up we go." The Boss would pull about five "G's" at the beginning of the loop which would bleed off as we approached the vertical and airspeed decreased. In an effort to make the smoke trail appear to be round instead of egg shaped, the Boss would call "Ease the pull" followed by "Comes the float" as we approached the inverted position. As the noses of the jets tracked below the horizon and airspeed increased, the Boss would call "Ease the power" and then say "Comes the pull" to complete the loop with about five "G's" at the bottom. On that fateful morning, over the California desert, this is how the loop actually went.

The first half of the loop was normal and as we reached the inverted position on top of the loop, the #2 pilot radioed he was a little flat (close) and was coming down. That's a signal for #3 and #4 to ease it out to make some room. Shortly after that transmission, I found myself (#3) flying on a fireball, a huge fuel/air explosion. There are specific emergency procedures for each maneuver and in this case, #4, the slot pilot, had to leave the formation before I could safely maneuver my jet to get clear of the other jets. All members of the Blue Angels are perfectionists but our slot pilot that year was an extremely demanding perfectionist. His name was Mike and when he came up on the radio to call clear, his voice was dripping with sarcasm and disgust as he said "One of you guys is on fire, Mike's clear." I remember thinking at the time, "Come on Mike, give us a break, we're on fire here." After Mike was clear, I was then able to maneuver my jet away from the other jets and recover from the maneuver. By this time, my jet was 90 degrees nose down, heading straight

### BY THE GRACE OF GOD

for the ground and accelerating. I checked airspeed and altitude and began the pull out. When I pulled back on the stick, however, the aircraft did not respond and remained in a 90 degree nose down attitude while accelerating at a rapid rate. At this point, I scanned the instruments checking for fire warning lights, hydraulic pressures and the mirrors, looking for evidence of fire. There were no anomalies except for the apparent flight control failure. And then, something extraordinary occurred. It was as if time stopped and, in my mind's eye, all I could see was a chart I used often in Viet Nam to determine the minimum ejection altitude above ground level (AGL) versus airspeed and dive angle. Just recently, I searched the internet for the F-4 NATOPS (Operations) manual and found the exact chart that had come to mind. When I found the chart, it sent chills down my back when I confirmed the numbers that had come to my mind, indicating I was passing through the minimum ejection altitude to safely egress from the jet. The chart is shown below.

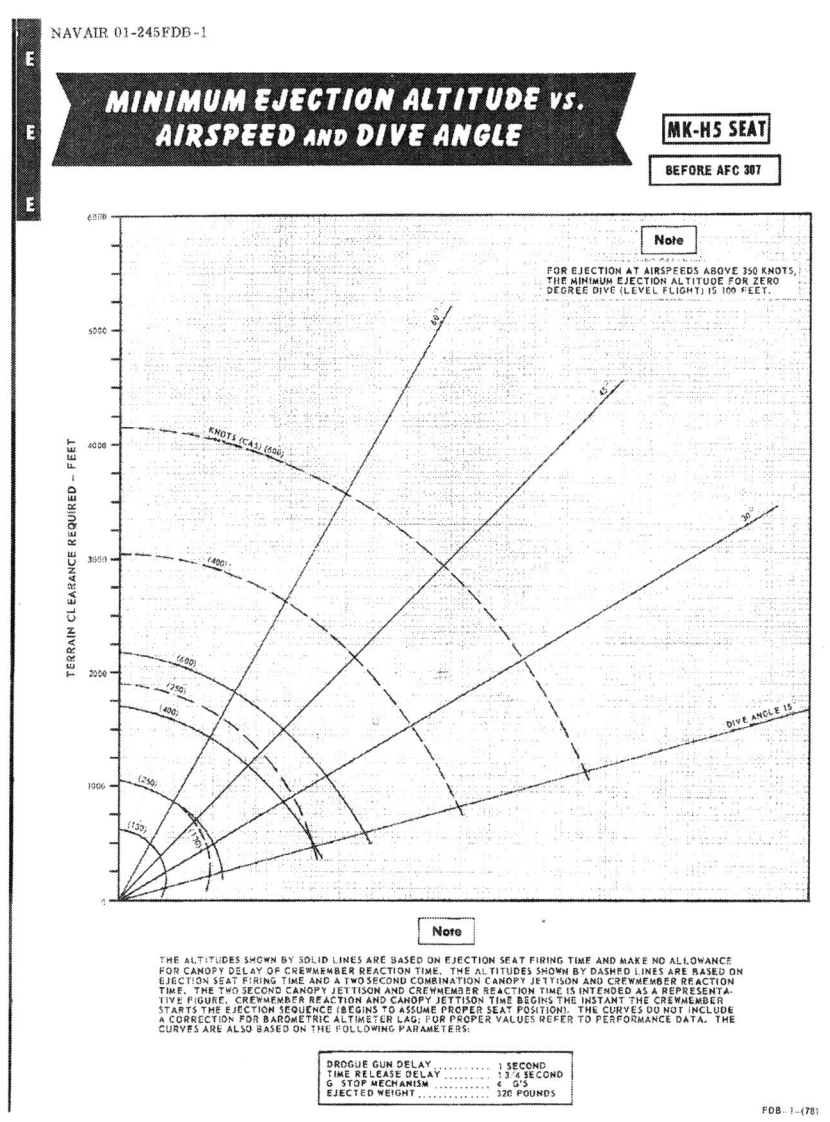

This chart is an official graph produced for the U.S. Navy and is public domain.

◄ **BY THE GRACE OF GOD**

I remember looking at the numbers on the chart and the minimum ejection altitude was around 3,400 feet AGL. Just a side note, there is no way I would have remembered the detail of that chart. I never attempted to memorize it. The point is, in my opinion, it was Divine intervention. I checked my airspeed which was 435 knots and increasing rapidly. The altimeter showed me passing 3,500 feet MSL, still in a 90 degree nose down attitude and to make things worse, the F-4 altimeter was known to lag by about 500 feet at this attitude and airspeed. Tactical jet pilots spend a lot of time training for the possibility of having to perform a "live" ejection. There are ejection seat simulators that give you a sense of what an ejection sequence might feel like but nothing can prepare you for the real thing. Between 400 and 500 KTS, it is likely you will suffer a flail injury of your arms because of the high speed ejection but you don't worry about that. If you are in uncontrolled flight and at the edge of the ejection envelope, the decision to eject is easy. If you don't, the only alternative is that you die. I knew I was out of time and needed to initiate ejection but we flew the Phantom with full nose down trim and if I let go of the stick to use both hands to pull the face curtain to initiate ejection, there was a chance the jet would pull some negative "G", even with the flight control failure. Even though the ejection seat was equipped with negative "G" restraints, you don't want an ejection seat to get a running start on your tailbone so I pulled the secondary ejection handle between my legs while continuing to hold the stick with my right hand. The first step in the ejection sequence is jettison of the canopy followed by sequential detonation of three pancake charges that propel the seat up the rails. While the pancake charges are firing, the seat occupant

## THE EL CENTRO MISHAP

is feeling about 23 "G's". After traveling a short distance, leg restraints immobilize your legs to prevent flail injuries in high speed ejections and then a rocket is ignited (about 15 "G's" sustained during the rocket burn) to propel the seat to an altitude where seat/man separation and chute deployment can be successful, even if the jet is on the ground (zero airspeed and zero altitude). All of this happens in about 1.5 seconds. The Blues fly with lip microphones and gold plated nuclear flash visors so you can still see while looking directly at the sun. On this morning, however, there was a high overcast so I was flying with my visor retracted. As the ejection seat started to exit the jet and my head was exposed to the slipstream at about 450 KTS, the lip microphone was pressed so hard against my chin that it left a blood blister impression of the microphone that persisted for a couple of weeks. The slip stream also ripped my helmet off and the helmet acted as a small parachute pulling sharply on my throat. Fortunately, the chin strap didn't fail and I was able to put the helmet back on prior to impact with the ground. Seat/man separation was normal but the chute opening was violent because of the airspeed at ejection. After deceleration, I saw my jet out in front of me with an aft section fuel fire. An aft section fuel fire occurs when fuel is streaming out of the fuel cell system and is somehow ignited. A moment later, it crashed into the desert floor.

While hanging in the chute, I began to assess the situation and discovered several of my parachute panels had been blown out due to the high speed ejection. The net effect of that is an increase in the rate of descent so the landing can be a little harder and more difficult to do without injury. I deployed the seat pan which contains a raft, oxygen and survival gear as a normal procedure, even over land. As you can imagine, my mind was racing, wondering about the fate of the other pilots and what impact this event would have on the future of the Blues. As to my fate, I thought survival was no longer an issue and that I would live through this experience but it wasn't over yet. As the descent toward the desert floor continued, it was very quiet, almost eerie, until parts of the #1 and #2 jets started raining down around me. Nose cones, outboard wing panels, ejection seats, canopies and a variety of other parts were falling from about 7,000 feet above me and needless to say, if any one of them had fallen in my chute, it would not have been a good day. Fortunately, none did and the landing was a little hard as expected and my head hit the ground with a "thump." We had a crew on the ground that videotaped the events of that day and they jumped in their truck and came to pick me up. As we were driving back to the center point I realized my back was injured and I had to lift my weight off my spine to relieve the pain.

An aircraft mishap investigation was begun immediately in an effort to determine the cause of the accident. Clearly, at least two and perhaps all three of the jets had collided. The question is why. The first step was to carefully study the video of the crash. The Blues always record a video of all airshows and practice airshows so there might be some clues as to what happened. On top of the trail loop with the jets inverted, two puffs of white smoke were visible followed shortly by a fireball. You could see the #4 jet clear the formation and my jet, #3 could be seen coming out of the formation heading straight for the ground. The video ended at that point. To see if any further

## THE EL CENTRO MISHAP

information could be obtained from the video, the Navy sent it to NASA's Jet Propulsion Laboratory (JPL). At that time, they had the most advanced imagining technology available in the world. I was never told the outcome of their analysis of the video. Obviously, many parts of the airplanes had fallen to the desert floor so the next step would be to plot the exact location of each of those pieces to see if that provided any clues as to the cause of the accident. More on that later. Pilot error could certainly be a cause but in this case, the #2 pilot had made a call that he was a "a little flat and coming down." The #3 and #4 response to that call was to move further away. So the formation was actually expanding or getting further away from each other when the fireball occurred. Further analysis of the debris field revealed an anomaly that could explain the cause of the fireball. The starboard aft dye missile carried on the #1 jet was found disassociated with the majority of the debris field so it must have fallen from the jet before the main collision. The hypothesis was that the missile came off the lead jet and hit the top or turtle back of the #2 jet. Fuel cells and hydraulic lines are located in that area of the jet which could account for the initial fireball. If the hydraulic line were cut, the #2 jet would have lost pitch control which could have contributed to a full blown mid-air between #1 and #2. The video did show #2 coming out of the fireball in uncontrolled flight in very close proximity to my jet, #3, but I felt no impact. There is only speculation as to how my jet ended up with an aft section fuel fire. As I mentioned earlier, the three pilots ejected safely and in the end, the accident investigation board listed all the possible causes but concluded, based on the available data, that the cause of the accident was "Undetermined."

## ◂ BY THE GRACE OF GOD

Three of us ejected that day and everyone survived but the Boss injured his back in the ejection and had to be replaced. I have often reflected on this sequence of events and wondered especially about the human mind's ability, in stressful situations, to recall highly detailed information in a split second. If that minimum ejection altitude chart had not come to mind, I might not have survived to tell this story. Divine intervention? I think so. The next story I want to tell also involves the Blue Angels and unfortunately, this mishap cost the lives of two pilots and one crew chief.

CHAPTER 3

# The Lakehurst Mishap

WE BRIEFED AT NAS Pensacola for a 1:00 PM departure for NAS Lakehurst, NJ with a refueling stop at Naval Air Station (NAS) Oceana. We left Pensacola with five F-4J Phantoms and discovered a hydraulic leak in the #2 jet at Oceana so we briefed our arrival maneuvers for just 4 jets at Lakehurst. Upon arrival at Lakehurst, we circled the field briefly to ID our checkpoints on the ground and began our arrival maneuvers. We began with a Diamond Head-On Pass with the Boss in the lead, lead solo on the right wing, I was on the left wing and #4 was in the slot position. After the head on pass, the solo pilot detached from the diamond and the slot pilot moved up to the right wing. We now have three jets in the formation and we set up behind the crowd for a Little V 360. Little V means there are three jets in the formation with #1 in the lead with the wingmen on the left and right wing of the leader. 360 refers to the degrees of arc we would fly through to complete the maneuver. The Diamond 360 and Little V 360 are the tightest formations the team flies, sometimes as close as 18 inches wingtip to canopy, and we completed

### BY THE GRACE OF GOD

the maneuver without any comments or problems. The next maneuver was the Little V roll which is considered to be the least difficult of all the diamond maneuvers. The entry seemed normal to me but that is based on feel alone. When you are flying 36" from another jet, there is no opportunity to look in the cockpit to check airspeed or anything else. You are literally focusing on rivets in the fuselage on the lead jet to maintain your position. The Boss called "Up we go" to begin the pull to position the formation with the correct nose up attitude to begin the roll. The Boss radioed the command to begin the roll by saying "OOH K" and we began the Little V roll to the left. When we reached the inverted position, the Boss transmitted "Keep it rolling" which was unusual at this point in the maneuver. The aerodynamic loops of each aircraft can be felt by all the airplanes in the formation and the leader's roll rate is determined to a great extent by the proximity of the wingmen to the leader's wing tips. In response to the leader's call to keep it rolling, I flew a deeper position, increasing the distance from my cockpit to the lead's wing tip and the right wingman flew a flatter (closer) position to help push the leader around the roll. As we neared completion of the roll but still nose low, the leader called "It's gonna be low (the bottom), don't sag (don't go low)." It didn't occur to me then but as I write these words now, I realize the call not to sag should have been a huge red flag about how really low we were going to be. We were still nose low on the recovery and I began to feel airframe buffet which means we were at a higher angle of attack than normal at this point in the maneuver (The leader was pulling more "G's" than normal or our airspeed was less than normal at this point in the maneuver).

## THE LAKEHURST MISHAP

The Phantom has outboard wing panels with dihedral that stall at 16 unit's angle of attack and higher. The fact that we were experiencing buffet would indicate we were above 16 units angle of attack and that the outboard wing panels had lost lift or were fully stalled. The F-4 has a notch in the lift curve that makes it possible to increase the angle of attack past 16 units and lift production actually decreases. The leader made another call not to sag on the bottom of the pull out. In my peripheral vision, I saw the formation descend below what later turned out to be tree tops. I saw a flash of light coming from the right wingman and it turned out it was the right wingman's crew chief ejecting. We had made the bottom of the maneuver and the noses were coming up and I thought we were going to make it but the lead jet shuddered and rolled to the left toward my aircraft. I broke away to the left and pulled the nose up, added power and rolled inverted to see what had happened. The lead was rolling to the left and crashed almost immediately and I didn't see any ejection attempts from my vantage point. The right wingman flew on for about 8/10 of a mile and crashed and I saw no ejection attempt from the #2 aircraft. It was a terrible thing to watch unfold. One of the characteristics screened for before being accepted as a student Naval Aviator is the ability of your mind to compartmentalize. This means you must be able to focus on the task at hand without allowing emotion or distractions to interfere with the successful completion of your mission or the operation of your aircraft. This is an essential characteristic of a combat pilot. Please understand, the loss I experienced that day and the emotion associated with it would manifest itself as time passed. I was the aviation safety officer for the team so I landed my jet and began the notification procedures for an aircraft mishap. Due to the high visibility of the Team, an operational report (OPREP 3) call had to be made immediately to inform the chain of command of the accident and status of the aircrews. The officer on duty was shocked by the news and notified the Secretary of the Navy immediately. A mishap investigation was begun and this is what they found.

So far as I could tell, the entry into the "Little V Roll" was normal but as I mentioned before, the wingmen are totally focused on maintaining their position on the lead aircraft, trying to remain within 6 inches of the prescribed bearing line and distance. There is no opportunity to look in the cockpit to check instruments. Once the formation was in the inverted position, the Boss called "Keep it rolling" which is a very unusual call at that point in the maneuver. The accident investigation board concluded the maneuver may have started a little slow, resulting in a slower than normal roll rate and a lower than normal altitude when the formation was in the inverted position. If that was the case, it would explain the Boss's subsequent calls indicating the bottom of the maneuver would be low. As we reached the bottom of the roll, I saw in my peripheral vision what turned out to be tree tops above us and it was then that the crew chief in the #2 jet ejected (that was the flash of light I saw at the bottom of the maneuver), believing we were about to impact the ground. His ejection seat left the aircraft but was out of the envelope for a safe ejection and he never got seat/man separation and struck a tree and/or impacted the ground while still in the seat and he was killed immediately.

## THE LAKEHURST MISHAP

At that point, I saw some movement of the #2 jet and the lead began to slowly roll towards my jet. Given our proximity to the ground, I could not maintain position and broke out of the formation to the left, pulled the nose up while adding power and then rolled inverted to see what was transpiring. The lead continued the roll to the left and initiated ejection while in a 90 degree right wing down attitude. The lead's crew chief came out of the aircraft but never got seat/man separation, passed through tree tops and hit the ground while still in the ejection seat. I believe there were at least a couple of miracles that day, but this one takes the cake. The lead's crew chief got seat/man separation when the seat hit the ground and he got up and walked away from the crash. The airspeed at the time of ejection had to be between 400 and 450 KTS or as much as 518 MPH. The lead aircraft continued to roll to the left and the pilot's ejection seat never left the #1 jet and the lead pilot was killed when the aircraft impacted the ground. The #2 jet flew on for 8/10 of a mile and crashed. Ejection was never initiated and the pilot was killed on impact.

The accident investigation team cited the following from several witnesses: "Numerous witnesses observed the formation descend below a tree line then come back up into sight." and "The aircraft were below the level of the trees at bottom-out." The investigation team also noted "The formation was in a flight situation which precipitated the aircraft collision with the trees." I was flying the left wing through the entire maneuver and was to the left and slightly below the lead aircraft which was documented to have struck one or more trees prior to initiating ejection. After landing, I conducted a post flight inspection of

◄ **BY THE GRACE OF GOD**

my jet, paying special attention to any possible evidence of tree strikes on any part of the airframe. There were none. The fact that my jet incurred no damage on the bottom out is highly improbable. I didn't think much about that then but in recent years I have concluded something more was at work than just luck or good piloting skills. I believe God intervened in my case and the lead crew chief's case and that we are alive today because of it. The loss of life at Lakehurst was tragic and it set in motion a sequence of events that would change the Blue Angels forever.

CHAPTER 4

# The Blue Angels in Transition

NINETEEN SEVENTY-THREE WAS a tragic year for the Blue Angels and the USAF Thunderbirds. The Blues lost six aircraft and three lives and the Thunderbirds experienced three mishaps that year. Both teams were flying the F-4 Phantom with each jet consuming 10,000 pounds of jet fuel per airshow. 1973 was also the year of the oil embargo and the entire country was experiencing a shortage of gasoline. It was particularly bad in the northeast and in California where people couldn't buy enough gas to drive to work. As a result, we were often met by members of the media upon arrival at new airshow sites with questions about how much fuel the F-4 burned. Further, the loss of lives and aircraft that both teams experienced prompted congress to question the value of the teams' mission and they directed the Department of Defense to conduct a cost/benefit analysis. It was determined that the flight demonstration teams had a huge positive effect on recruiting for both officer and enlisted ranks and that it would cost more than the teams' budgets if you had to use conventional advertising to obtain the same results. So the decision was made to continue operation of the demonstration teams but a transition to much more fuel efficient airplanes was directed. As a result, the Blues transitioned to the A-4 Skyhawk and the Thunderbirds transitioned to the T-38 Talon.

In the second half of 1973, with input from the Blues, the Navy selected the A-4's to be modified for use in airshows. In order for an airplane to be effective in the airshow business, it must be capable of generating smoke and the fuel system and ejection seat have to be modified to allow for sustained negative "G" flight. In the case of the A-4, the leading edge slats had to be bolted up as well. And, of course, the planes had to be repainted with the classic Blue Angel color scheme. So, by the end of 1973, the Team had eight single seat A-4's and one two seat A-4 for the narrator to provide media rides at the airshow sites.

Another major change for the Team was the implementation of a transition from the Team or Detachment status to a full blown Squadron status. This was as a result of the aircraft mishap investigation team recommendation that a flight surgeon be assigned to the squadron on a full time basis. The 1973 airshow schedule included an Atlantic crossing to Europe where we flew airshows in England, France, Spain, Turkey, Iran and Italy. That deployment lasted a full month. We were supposed to have a week off upon our return to the States but the State Department wrote in an unscheduled airshow in the Bahamas in celebration of the Bahamas Independence Day. The investigation team concluded that the 1973 airshow schedule was too extensive and that pilot fatigue was a contributing factor in the NAS Lakehurst accident. The thought was that a flight surgeon

## THE BLUE ANGELS IN TRANSITION

would recognize the symptoms of fatigue where a pilot might not. So the Navy Flight Demonstration Squadron departed for El Centro, California in early January 1974.

The A-4 was much more maneuverable than the F-4 and it was much easier to fly in the airshow business. Because of its shorter turn radius, you could keep the show tighter and have a maneuver in front of the crowd almost continually. As a result, winter training went very well and the entire 1974 airshow schedule was completed without any mishaps or accidents of any kind.

*A-4 Skyhawk.   Photo by Ron Rentfrow.   Blue Angel diamond landing.*

Now I want to tell you about a very personal story that changed my life for the better and share some insights into what it is like to get married while flying as a demonstration pilot with the Blue Angels.

CHAPTER 5

# Out of the Blue

IT WAS THE summer of 1974 and we were almost half way through the airshow season. I was a member of the Pensacola Yacht Club and spent as much time there as I could when we were not on the road. It was there that I met this girl. I thought she was the most beautiful girl I had ever seen. I had seen her on other sailboats while racing but I never had the chance to meet her until May of '74. We started dating and before long, we were spending all our free time together when I was in town. Her name was Pat and she was able to come to a few airshows during the airshow season and one of those was our show at NAS Oceana the weekend of July 27. Pat and I grew very fond of each other very quickly which I had not anticipated. I was going to be 30 years old in December and I had resigned myself to the possibility I might not find "the one" anytime soon. I titled this chapter "Out of the Blue" because once I got to know Pat well it was as if she had hit me between the eyes with a 2 X 4. I knew she was "the one" and I had fallen in love. Earlier in the month, I had taken Pat out on a sailboat on Pensacola Bay with the intent of asking her

### BY THE GRACE OF GOD

to marry me. We both loved sailing and I thought that would be the perfect place to ask for her hand in marriage. I had the ring and somehow it just didn't feel like the "right" time so I chickened out. The weather at NAS Oceana was terrible with rain forecast for the entire weekend. We kept hoping it would improve so we could fly the shows but it didn't and we ended up with time on our hands. I had been carrying the ring with me and Pat and I were having a great time so I decided I just couldn't wait. I asked Pat if she would marry me and she said "yes!" From that point forward, our visit to Oceana became a celebration and that night we had dinner with all the guys and champagne for all. Now you need to understand something about the Blues.

Getting married while you are assigned to the Blues presents some challenges. We wanted to get married on a Saturday so we couldn't do that until the airshow season was over. So we picked December 7th, 1974 as the date for our wedding. One of the benefits of being married on Pearl Harbor Day is that it would be highly improbable that I would ever forget our anniversary. Another thing I was told were stories of things the Blues of the past have done to guys getting married while on the Team. Some of the stories are pretty radical (all in good fun) and I don't know for sure if these stories are true but it planted a seed that I couldn't ignore. You can imagine, as our wedding day approached, I remained at a level of high alert.

A few weeks prior to the wedding, Pat and I got some intelligence from a friend who was close to the Sheriff of Escambia

County. The Sheriff had agreed to arrest me at my bachelor party. It was time to go to general quarters so I contacted a friend of mine at the Yacht Club who was head of the FBI locally. I told him what the Sheriff planned to do so he contacted a friend of his who happened to be a Federal judge. The judge issued a Writ of Habeas Corpus which is the fundamental instrument for safeguarding individual freedom against arbitrary and lawless state action. The Federal judge made it a Federal crime for any state law enforcement officer to arrest me from midnight the day before our wedding to midnight the day after our wedding. My FBI friend agreed to attend the party to enforce the Writ so we thought we had the legal part covered. I was still concerned about someone putting a sedative in my drink at the bachelor party so I asked another friend who was a physician to attend the party equipped with antidotes for any sedative they might try to use (rumors were that had happened in the past). He agreed to attend also. And finally, just for icing on the cake, I asked a friend who was about 6'8" tall and weighed 320 pounds to be my bodyguard. He agreed. Pat's friends were having a bachelorette party for her at Trader Jon's, a famous watering hole in downtown Pensacola. It was a very popular bar with the military and Trader Jon was a friend of ours. He promised to personally take care of Pat and her friends so we weren't so concerned for Pat. So, Pat and I thought we had the bases covered for the bachelor parties and the wedding. But not so fast.

The night of the bachelor party, all my friends were in place and I had the Writ of Habeas Corpus in my pocket. Someone gave me a drink at the party and it had a very strange taste so

◂ BY THE GRACE OF GOD

I threw it out. So, all was going well until the Sheriff's deputies showed up. They made it clear they were going to arrest me so I stood up on a chair and proudly read the Writ to everybody in attendance. The deputies didn't care and arrested me anyway and took me to the county jail. My FBI guy decided to let the prank play out so I knew I was toast. When we arrived at the jail, they put me through the finger printing and mug shot process with me protesting the whole time. I found out after the fact that one of the deputies was not in on the game and he almost beat me with his night stick. Anyway, after a few hours in the slammer, my FBI guy showed up, sprung me out of jail and gave me a ride back to the house where they held the bachelor party. Of one thing I was sure…these guys were not finished yet.

The Blue Angels have a long tradition of the "Dead Fortis." Once one of the Team members gets "loaded" (I'll explain that in a minute), he can call "Dead Ant" and all the officers of the Team are to fall on their backs with their hands and feet in the air as fast as they can. The last person down is required to buy a round of drinks for all the officers within a certain period of time and when that's been done, he is loaded and may call "Dead Ant" at any time. Over the years, two situations were identified that were exceptions to the rule and you were prohibited from calling "Dead Ant" in those situations. The first exception is while airborne. Years ago, someone actually called a "Dead Ant" while the Team was in route to a show site and everybody responded by rolling their jets to the inverted position at 28,000 feet. They decided that was a bad idea so that practice was banned. The second exception is when everyone is in a restroom. Use your imagination. I think the reason for that ban is obvious. The purpose of this tradition is not clear except everyone seems to enjoy it, both on and off the Team. In a way, it humanizes the demonstration pilots and is certainly an ice breaker. "Dead Ant" has been called in almost every circumstance you can think of but the one that stands out the most in my mind was in the Eiffel Tower in Paris. We were there for the Paris Airshow and were attending a reception in the Tower with dignitaries from governments, major aerospace corporations, the military and others. At some point, they gathered us all together for a picture and one of our guys called the "Dead Ant" and we all went down. These people were very senior people from countries all around the world and some were sworn enemies. At first, they seemed confused but then they all laughed and great conversations ensued. It certainly made the situation a lot less stuffy. Now let me tell you why I am giving you this background.

Two or three weeks prior to our wedding, one of the guys was "loaded" and he made the call. I made sure I was the last one down and bought drinks for everyone immediately. I wanted to make sure I was "loaded" on our wedding day. The officers of the Squadron had all agreed to be part of our wedding party and one of their duties is to form a sword arch that the newly married couple walks through after the wedding ceremony. That passage is meant to ensure the couple's safe transition into their new life together. After our wedding and the final blessing, Pat and I walked arm in arm up the aisle to the entrance of the church and all the guys were there in full dress uniforms ready to form the sword arch. The Boss gave the

## BY THE GRACE OF GOD

command to draw swords and they formed the arch of swords for us to walk through. When we reached the end of the arch, I performed an about face and assumed the position of parade rest and made the call "Dead ant!" All the officers immediately fell to the ground with their covers (hats) flying everywhere but the senior Marine C-130 pilot had a problem. He lost control of his sword and it went flying through the air end over end. I held my breath as I watched the sword, not knowing where it might land. The sword finally hit the concrete landing squarely on its point and then came to rest on its side. By the grace of God, it didn't land on somebody. That would have really been a bad start to our marriage. The pictures below say it all.

*Photo by Charles Massey*

*Photo by Charles Massey*

After everyone recovered from the dead ant, we all proceeded to the reception but Pat and I anticipated the Team would attempt to mess with us somehow so we made plans accordingly.

We assumed the guys would try to do something before we left the reception so we came up with a plan to foil whatever they might be planning. A friend of ours arranged for a limousine to take us to and from the reception so when it came time to leave, he was briefed to blow by the entrance to the building, stop briefly and Pat and I would run out, jump in the car and he would speed off. Our friend drove us to the airport as quickly as possible where we were met by another friend, Chipper, who was a pilot and owned a twin engine airplane. We were going to the Bahamas on our honeymoon and we didn't want

### BY THE GRACE OF GOD

the Blues to know that until after the fact. No telling what they might try to do if they knew. When we arrived at the fixed base operation (FBO), the airplane and pilot were waiting on the ramp with engines running. So, to confuse the guys, Chipper filed a flight plan to New Orleans where we spent the night. The next morning, Pat and I boarded a commercial flight to the Bahamas and enjoyed a great honeymoon cruise on the 282′ four masted bark, Fantome. We took great delight in sending several post cards to the guys just to rub it in a little. Five years after we were married, Pat and I found ourselves in a survival situation we will never forget.

So far, you have read two survival stories and here's another that involved Pat, myself and a friend. Pat and I took delivery of a new Mariner 36 racing/cruising sailboat in the summer of 1979. Within a few weeks of taking delivery, hurricane Frederic came ashore near Gulf Shores, Alabama as a category 4 storm with winds at 145 MPH. We could not leave he boat at the dock and expect it to survive. So Pat and I and a friend, took the boat to sea in the face of the hurricane and this is our survival story.

CHAPTER **6**

# Hurricane Frederic

HURRICANE FREDERIC ROARED ashore at Gulf Shores, Alabama on September 12, 1979 and the following is a true story. This was written in 1985 and I feel it's a tale that needs to be told so that other yachting enthusiasts might learn from our mistakes and our successes. Pat and I have been racing sailboats since 1971 and have owned five racer/cruisers; we've watched spinnakers explode in gale force winds and without concern flown another. But, I was not prepared for the raw force of this storm. I'm a Marine Corps fighter pilot with 200 combat missions in Viet Nam and an ex-Blue Angel pilot and Top Gun graduate. I've been exposed to many life threatening situations and I've always felt in control until now. For me, Hurricane Frederic dispelled that illusion once and for all.

On September the 12th, 1979, a category 4 hurricane named Frederic slammed ashore on the Gulf Coast at Gulf Shores, Alabama and caused more destruction of property than can be described. It was the most destructive and costly hurricane in U.S. history at that time. Pat and I had purchased a new Mariner 36 in January of that year and were living

◀ **BY THE GRACE OF GOD**

in Pensacola, Florida. The Mariner 36 is a very capable off shore cruising and racing sail boat. It is well designed and we equipped it to be able to handle most anything that we might experience while racing and cruising in the open ocean. We had given some thought to what we might do in the event of a hurricane but we had never really considered the sequence of events which lead up to the arrival of a hurricane and to how much would have to be done to protect ourselves, our boat and other property. I guess most people wait until the last minute before they start to prepare for a storm because the chances of the weather service accurately predicting where a storm is going ashore is really dismal (in 1979) until 24 hours prior to the forecast landfall. In our case, Pat and I planned to meet at the Yacht Club for lunch and when I arrived, she informed me that the hurricane was forecast to hit Pensacola in 36 hours. So, at 12 noon on Wednesday, the clock started ticking for us and our boat, the Foggy Daze.

As luck would have it, our new VHF radio had failed the previous week. So I set out to find a new radio while Pat began to gather provisions. Mariner's President had graciously sent Steve, Mariner's customer service V.P. to Pensacola to make some modifications to our boat (unsolicited but greatly appreciated, I might add) and he stayed aboard completing some last minute work. I returned to the boat with the new radio and antenna and Steve and I installed it quickly while Pat loaded provisions. We finished removing everything possible from the deck and rigging and duct taped everything else that could flail in the wind, while Steve made his escape good on the last airplane to leave Pensacola before the storm.

# HURRICANE FREDERIC

It's now 2000 (8:00 PM) on Wednesday evening and Pat and I left the boat to secure our house and 9' Boston Whaler dinghy and deliver our two miniature pincers to Pat's parent's house where they were convinced that we had lost our minds. I wonder what makes two reasonably normal people take 22,000 pounds of boat into 145 KTS of wind when the thing is fully insured. I guess I'll never know for sure. We got back to the boat at 0300 (3:00 AM) on Thursday morning and the winds and tide were on the rise. There was no way we were going to get any sleep at this point, so we decided to shower and have a cocktail instead. That completed, Pat and I made some last minute preparations while we waited for Donnie to arrive. Donnie is a friend of ours whom we invited to a hurricane party...and he came. Donnie arrived at 0500 (5:00 AM) and we got underway shortly thereafter as the rising tide began to lap at the top of the dock. As we motored into Pensacola Bay, I looked over my shoulder at Pensacola Yacht Club with its southeast exposure to the Bay and knew that any boat berthed there was going to be in serious trouble.

As we crossed Pensacola bay, the wind and seas were increasing rapidly and by the time we got to the mouth of the Bay, Gulf waves were breaking across the low lying beach. The storm had been trending to the west but we couldn't go east due to bridges and our mast height and the rising tide. We continued west with the intent of anchoring in the protected waters of Ingram's Bayou. In route, we stopped at the Shelter Cove Marina to take on fuel. The owner invited us to tie up there, since the marina was on the Intracoastal Waterway and in very protected waters. I didn't want to be anywhere near a dock so I declined politely, and we moved on. It is a five hour trip from the yacht club to Ingram's Bayou so we arrived at 10:30 AM and found six other sailboats already anchored. The only place we could find with enough swinging room placed us to weather of all the boats and in a slightly more exposed position. The weather guessers were now saying the storm was going to make landfall near Gulf Shores, Alabama which was due south of our anchorage. With the storm tracking 350 degrees, there was a good chance the eye of the storm would pass over us so we were forced to anchor Bahamian style with our two largest anchors (One anchor set up-wind and secured to the bow and another anchor secured to the bow and the anchor is set down-wind off the stern of the boat). Just in case the weather guys were all wet, we put out our lunch hook (a small anchor), a Danforth 13, to the north in case Frederic passed to the east of our position. So there we are, a 35 plow deployed to the northeast into the wind, a Danforth 20H to the southwest in case the eye passed overhead, and a Danforth 13S to the north in case everybody was wrong. Our friends Murdock and Bob were on board their boats and both were very experienced sailors so if the eye of the storm passed over us we were comfortable that we wouldn't have to worry about Murdock or Bob. The unmanned boats were a serious concern if the eye hit us because unmanned boats tend to drag anchors and chafe through lines without a crew onboard.

We checked some last minute things; made sure the chafe gear was in place; secured the bitter ends of the anchor lines to the base of the mast (stepped on the keel); ran safety lines fore and aft/port and starboard; checked our safety gear, flares, harnesses, knives, hand guns for the indigenous alligators, in case we were beached, and generally made ready for the storm.

Pat made radio contact with the other boats in the anchorage and tried to rest. The shrimp boat captains, realizing we would probably take a direct hit from the storm, began talking among themselves about the possibility of getting the Coast Guard to pick them up. One of the more senior captains came up on the radio and quite properly told the other shrimpers there was no chance the Coast Guard would put to sea at this point in the storm. Pat tried to get me to sleep while I could, and I should have, but you try to sleep when you're anchored on your new boat right in the path of a major hurricane with your wife and a friend on board and six boats to leeward. At this point, the cloud formations were very interesting and also a concern.

◄ BY THE GRACE OF GOD

*Hurricane Frederic*  *Photo by NOAA*

At our anchorage, we still had blue sky and fair weather. But as the storm approached, the outer bands of clouds became very evident and they were very tightly wrapped which did not bode well for us.

Have you ever noticed that stressful experiences in the night are worse than in the daytime, and have you ever noticed when hurricanes like to go feet dry? You got it...at night...they seem to slow down 50 or 60 miles off-shore, spool up a little, like a pitcher making his wind up for a fast ball, and then they race ashore, knock the hell out of you and, somehow, you get the feeling that the thing is enjoying every minute of it. Well, Frederic was no exception. Winds reached hurricane force at about 1800 (6:00 PM) and everything was going well until Don looked out a porthole at a stump and a tree we had been using for bearings to make sure we weren't dragging anchor. Our primary anchor was dragging and we were closing on the leeward boats slowly. Don and I scrambled on deck and made our way forward to pay out more rode in an attempt to set the anchor but with no luck. We were now hanging on the lunch hook with six feet of chain and 150 feet of half inch line so we payed out all of the 35 plow rode and secured the line in case the lunch hook should drag or part. I was going on deck every fifteen minutes to check for chafing and to check our position. The winds reached 85 kts by 2000 (8:00 PM) and the Danforth 13 was proving itself to be a remarkable anchor. Then, with a crack like a shot, the lunch hook line parted and the Foggy Daze fell off before the wind and accelerated to hull speed (1.34 times the square root of the waterline length or about 7.5 KTS) in a matter of seconds and bore sighted a Morgan 30-2 to leeward. The skipper of the Morgan, Bob and I clambered on deck as the 22,000 pound Foggy Daze prepared to almost assuredly send Bob and his boat to the bottom of the bayou. I managed to get to the foredeck prior to impact and looked into Bob's eyes and I could see the helplessness which he had to have seen in mine. And then, just prior to impact, I was thrown to the side as the Foggy Daze began to slow...the 20H we had set to leeward was taking strain and the 3/4" rode appeared to look more like 1/2" line as the boat heeled and threw her beam to an angered and disappointed storm. The storm was not to be denied so easily, however, as our anchor sprit penetrated the privacy of Bob's cockpit. The impact we feared became more of a respectful touch than a hull crushing catastrophe. The only damage was to our anchor roller guides which were butterflied with near perfect symmetry, obviously as a subtle hint to carry bigger anchors. But the danger was not past as our two boats looked like they were rafted together to engage in some social event rather than two boats and crews fighting for survival in a killer storm. We payed out all the remaining line on our 20H and that moved us astern of Bob's boat but our anchor line would ride under Bob's boat and hang on the keel and rudder as our boat sailed from side to side, a nasty habit most fin keel boats have in high winds at anchor. Fortunately, Bob is a racing sailor who keeps his bottom clean or our line would have chafed through in seconds because of barnacles attached to the hull of most boats. I went forward to check on the anchor and to my surprise and horror, found the rode nearly chafed through in less than fifteen minutes. The boat was so new we had never anchored it in high winds and we were unaware that the manufacturer had used hexagon bolts to secure the stem fitting to the hull. Those bolts acted just like a saw on the anchor lines, just like a hot knife through butter. (After the storm, those bolts were replaced with rounded head bolts. That solved the problem.) I could not pull the line in beyond the chafed area so it was likely we were going to lose that anchor in a few minutes and the only other anchor we had down was the 35 plow and it was dragging. Quickly, I went below and reluctantly told Pat and Don about what was happening as the winds increased to over 100 KTS. Pat asked me if we were going to make it and, with as much confidence as I could muster, I said "We'll make it." Somehow, the realization that we might be blown ashore, or worse yet, collide with boats to leeward gave us renewed determination to save the boat and along with it, ourselves. I manned the helm and started the engine to take strain off the anchor and to keep us away from Bob's boat while Pat called the other boats to let them know what was happening. Clearly, we had a chafing problem that had not been anticipated. The boat was sailing so badly by the bow that the anchor rode was being sawed in two by the stem fitting bolts on the bow. In a fit of inspiration, Don pulled out his survival knife and began to cut away some of the boat's hot water reinforced hose in lengths long enough to extend beyond the bow. Pat secured the fresh water pump while Don slit the hose end to end, grabbed some duct tape, and crawled to the foredeck. I began to feel like we were about to regain control of the situation when the rode on the 20H parted. The line was so stretched that the recoil carried it almost twenty meters against the wind toward Bob's boat and wrapped itself around his headstay. The storm drove the Foggy Daze to leeward. I began to look for a safe path to the leeward beach when our dragging 35 lb. plow decided to set once and for all.

Our situation was clearly tenuous as Pat manually inflated half of our dingy (The dingy had two air chambers and if she had inflated both chambers, it wouldn't have fit through the companionway.) and Don slid the hose over the rode of our

◂ BY THE GRACE OF GOD

last anchor, reinforcing it with duct tape for the entire length. Don spent the rest of the night on the bow taking up slack in the anchor line so I wouldn't foul the prop. Bob called on the radio and said he had secured our 20H rode to one of his cleats and asked if we wanted him to try to float the line to us. Since I was relying on the engine to take strain off the anchor line, I decided not to try to transfer the line for fear that it might foul the prop. The boat had enough power to relieve most of the strain on the anchor and the chafing gear seemed to be working well as the wind increased to over 130 KTS and the tidal surge rose fifteen feet above normal. There were times during the storm when the hull of the boat brushed the tops of medium size pine trees that had been on dry land when we first arrived in the Bayou. Our boat was being blown so hard that, even with bare poles, (no sails) the lee toe rail was underwater. By 2400 (midnight) the storm was at its worst, and I was becoming fatigued to the point that I began to see things that weren't there. I needed something for energy and Pat poured some Gatorade. However, by the time she could pass it to me in the cockpit, the venturi effect would suck the glass dry, so she gave me a small bag of sugar but it was nearly impossible to eat the stuff in 130 KT winds and blown water. At this point, we were in the right, front, advancing quadrant of the eye wall. There can be no worse place to be than that. We were experiencing the worst the storm had to offer.

At about 0200 (2:00 AM), Pat looked out of the cabin and at the same moment I began to hear a strange whistling noise. All of the sudden, Pat yelled, "get down!" I dropped into the cockpit behind the wheel and looked up to see a water spout rising out of the water just a few feet from the boat. Fortunately, it moved away downwind. Shortly after that, an unattended Westsail 32 was blown ashore while the tidal surge was still high. We were only one anchor away from a similar fate. Pat was being driven crazy by our ship's bell clock that would ring every 30 minutes to remind us of, not only the time, but of watch changes. The net effect of that was that time passed like molasses on a cold day. By 0400 (4:00 AM), the worst of the storm had passed and by sunrise, the clouds began to dissipate and the sun began to breathe new energy into my exhausted crew and me. With daylight, we could begin to see some of the effects of the storm. The Westsail 32 was standing upright in the trees with the base of its keel three feet out of the water on dry land. Almost half of the pine trees surrounding Ingram's Bayou had been blown down to a 45 degree angle and many had been uprooted entirely. As the weather continued to improve, we could finally begin to relax.

With the storm passed, we all decided to raft up and wait for the winds to dissipate further and to have breakfast. As I reflected on the events of the night, I realized Pat was the only female on any of the boats anchored there. I also realized I had the best wife and friend in the whole world. Pat had anticipated we might be stranded for several days so she had provisioned the boat well. She prepared a great and appreciated breakfast while I made some bloody marys. I don't believe you ever feel more alive than you do when you go through an experience like this. You never appreciate what

## BY THE GRACE OF GOD

you have until you almost lose it. We decided to head back to the Yacht Club at about 0900 (9:00 AM) but we couldn't get our 35 plow up. Once it set, it went "half way to China" so our good friend Murdock in his Choy Lee 40 lashed his boat to ours and with both engines at full power, we managed to break the anchor free. We left Ingram's Bayou and entered the Intracoastal Waterway just north of Gulf Shores, Alabama and found a scene that reminded me of a war zone. A One Ton racing boat was high and dry just to the west and as we looked to the east it was evident that mass destruction was the norm.

At this point, I went below to get something but I was so exhausted I fell asleep. So did Donnie. Therefore, from this point forward, what I'm describing is what Pat saw as she took the helm and navigated back to the yacht club. Many of the waterway marks had been completely destroyed or the floating marks had drug all over the place, so Pat had to make her way to the east based on her knowledge of where the channel was and not where the marks were. As we approached Shelter Cove Marina, the one where the owner had invited us to stay during the storm, she noticed a large powerboat barely breaking the surface of the water. We later discovered a lady had lost her life on that boat after it was holed and sunk. The Marina docks were almost completely destroyed and several boats were severely damaged. As we entered Grand Lagoon, the power of the storm became even more evident. Many homes had been destroyed along the waterfront. The barrier island had been cut in half and a 50' sailboat had been blown from the Gulf, across the Barrier

Island and Grand Lagoon then 30 meters on flooded land to eventually stick its keel in the front door of someone's house. We later heard the crew of that unfortunate boat decided to call it quits and went upstairs in the evacuated house and went to bed.

As we approached the Yacht Club, I woke up, went on deck and surveyed the situation. I was the Rear Commodore and Dock Chairman that year so what I saw made me feel sick. There were six boats that remained at the Yacht Club during the storm and five had been sunk. The docks were essentially unusable and extremely dangerous. As we tried to find a safe place to tie up, we noticed Pat's mother sitting at the base of the flagpole with an expression of relief and disbelief. After we met with Pat's mother, we were able to locate a slip at the Navy Yacht Club (NYC) which is a very safe harbor. We moved the Foggy Daze to NYC and Pat's mother picked us up. And so ends the chapter on hurricane Frederic.

If you should make the decision to stay on your boat during a storm, then I hope this tale will help you. If you have a choice, however, I recommend you make sure you've got good insurance, get the boat away from the dock, find a protected anchorage, put down some oversized ground tackle with good chafe gear and then go home. I, for one, have recognized my mortality. It is safe to say this could have ended very badly.

Just luck? I don't think so.

### ◄ BY THE GRACE OF GOD

Two weeks after the storm passed, Pat and I set sail for Ingram's Bayou once again, this time with Joyce and Keith, Pat's mother and father on board. We planned to anchor and have lunch and we towed our dingy and planned to drag hooks and try to recover the anchors we lost during the storm. Ground tackle like that is expensive and it's worth the effort to at least try. The damage caused by the storm was profound and the weather that day was beautiful and in such contrast to our experience two weeks earlier. We had a great lunch and told Pat's parents about all our experiences the night of Frederic. Soon, it came time to start dragging for the anchor lines. We brought a three pronged lead weighted grappling hook and started dragging where we thought the anchor lines would be on the bottom. Pat and I were shocked when we recovered both anchor lines on the first try. That made for a great end to a very pleasant day on the waters of northwest Florida and southern Alabama. Our boat, the "Foggy Daze" is pictured below.

HURRICANE FREDERIC

*Photo by Pat Fogg*

Now, let's talk about intuition.

# CHAPTER 7

# Intuition

THROUGHOUT MY LIFE, I have been intuitive and in some cases, it has saved my life. While intuition was not in play with the two mishaps and hurricane Frederic, it has been directly responsible for my taking action that ultimately saved my life. Let me give you some examples.

I was attending Butler University in Indianapolis, Indiana in 1965 and was pursuing a private pilot certificate in preparation for beginning flight training with the U.S. Marine Corps upon graduation. The Fixed Base Operator (FBO) was located on a one mile square grass field located on the Northwest side of town. I was renting a newly introduced Mooney Master with fixed landing gear and a variable pitch propeller.

One of the nice features of the airplane was a wing leveling system that allowed you to set power and trim for airspeed and the autopilot would keep the wings level and hold whatever heading you selected. After departure from the uncontrolled airfield on a solo cross country training flight, I set climb power, trimmed for climb airspeed and set the heading and engaged

## BY THE GRACE OF GOD

the wing leveling system. This allowed me to focus on the aviation charts that would guide me through the planned route. I was an inexperienced student pilot and I spent too much time "heads down" in the cabin reviewing the charts. At some point, I felt a strong need to do a scan outside the airplane and when I checked at 12 o'clock, I was a second or two from colliding with a 1,500' TV tower. I grabbed the yoke, disengaged the wing leveling system and rolled to 60 degrees right wing down and pulled, barely missing the radiating element on top the tower. Truly, if I had waited another second or two, I would not be here today. Now, let me give you three more examples where intuition certainly prevented serious injury or saved my life.

The year was 1968 and I was assigned to Advanced Jet Training in Kingsville, Texas. I was single, a 1st Lieutenant in the Marine Corps and my car was an XKE Jaguar Coup. I mention the car to make the point that it was a small two seat sports car, not one you would choose if you knew you were going to be in a collision. It was a Saturday night in south Corpus Christi and I was on my way back to the Bachelor Officer Quarters (BOQ) in Kingsville. I was driving west on a four lane highway and was stopped in the left lane at a red light and there was another car in the right lane, both waiting for the green light. I felt the need to check my rear view mirror and saw a single car in my lane closing on us at what appeared to be a very high rate of speed. The light was still red and it was clear the car was not decelerating and both lanes had cars in its path. At the last second, it became apparent the car was not slowing and it was about to rear end me at a high rate of speed. I floored the accelerator, threw it in 1st gear and popped the clutch while turning to the left to clear the lane. My car jumped through the red light into the intersection and fortunately no other cars were there. The speeding car flew through the intersection and the red light, barely missing my car and the car in the right lane. I decided I would try to get the license number of the speeding car so I cleared the intersection, steered back into the left lane and accelerated as fast as the car would go. Passing 100 miles per hour (not a smart decision) I was still not closing on the speeding car so I gave it up and slowed down to the speed limit. There is no doubt in my mind that if I had not checked my rear view mirror when I did and cleared the lane, the speeding car would have collided with me and given the other car's speed, I doubt I would have survived. Many years later in Pensacola, Pat and I had a very similar experience.

Pat and I were returning to Pensacola from Perdido Key on Gulf Beach Highway. It was about 10:00 PM and again, we were stopped at a red light at the intersection of Blue Angel Parkway and Gulf Beach Highway. Again, I felt the need to check the rear view mirror and a car was approaching and not slowing for the red light or us. It became obvious the car was not going to stop so, once again, I accelerated through the red light into the intersection while turning left to clear the lane. The approaching car apparently didn't see us or the red light and sped through the intersection, oblivious to what had just happened. In this case, we did catch up with the car when they stopped for another red light. It turned out to be two young women who were very fortunate not to have been injured on that dark night. Needless to say, Pat and I were very relieved at the outcome. The next experience I want to relate where intuition was in play

◄ BY THE GRACE OF GOD

happened while I was the Commanding Officer of VMFA 122 in Beaufort, South Carolina.

    VMFA 122 was an F-4 Phantom Squadron with 12 F-4's assigned. The F-4 was designed as a high altitude, high speed and high thrust to weight ratio aircraft but it was not highly maneuverable in the air to air combat role. So, F-4 aircrews had to develop combat tactics that focused on the strengths of the Phantom. One of the tactics developed to counter high altitude bombers and fighter aircraft was the supersonic snap-up. Enemy pilots approaching a target at high altitude in the range of 30,000 to 40,000 feet had a limited field of vision at 12:00 o'clock below the nose and their look down radar was handicapped by background clutter when scanning below the horizon. The supersonic snap-up was designed to take advantage of those weaknesses. The F-4 attacking aircrew would approach the target at low altitude, around 5,000 feet or lower, and accelerate to 1.2 MACH (1.2 times the speed of sound). Another F-4 would simulate the enemy aircraft by climbing to over 30,000 feet and the two fighters would separate by 20 miles and then vector towards each other for the attack. The radar intercept officer (RIO) in the F-4 simulating the enemy aircraft would try to acquire the attacking F-4 using the onboard Doppler radar which was capable of seeing velocity as well as reflected radar energy. The attacking F-4 would acquire the enemy simulator as well and maneuver to intercept while optimizing the weapon system capabilities. Both the AIM 7 Sparrow (radar guided) and AIM 9 Sidewinder (heat seeking) were most lethal when launched with a look-up angle. So, with both aircraft at supersonic speeds, they would approach each other for a head on

## INTUITION

pass and simulate a FOX 1 (sparrow launch) or a FOX 2 (sidewinder launch). The radar in the F-4 provided a display where a dot on the screen, when centered in a circle, represented a collision course to the target and a variable diameter circle would cue the pilot and RIO as to the maximum and minimum launch parameters of the missile selected. In this case, I was the pilot of the attacking F-4 at low altitude and supersonic speed. The pilot of the enemy simulator was a relatively inexperienced 1st Lieutenant and his RIO was a very experienced officer. At about five miles to intercept, I selected full afterburner and pulled the nose up to about 30° above the horizon and centered the dot temporarily to maximize missile accuracy. The F-4 simulating the enemy aircraft was briefed to not center the dot to avoid a mid-air collision. As we were nearing the intercept point, I maneuvered the dot out of the circle and simultaneously experienced a strong intuition something was wrong. So I rolled the airplane upside down to get a visual on the other F-4. When you look down the longitudinal axis of an F-4 in full afterburner, you can see the heat signature of the afterburners as broiling superheated air behind the jet. It also meant the opposing aircraft was on a collision course with my F-4 with both of us at supersonic speed and less than a second to a mid-air collision. I rolled the airplane upright and pulled the stick into my lap, nearly stalling the airplane. As the two jets passed, we were so close to each other that the supersonic shock wave from my wingman hit my Phantom with such force I thought we might have actually made physical contact. I called to knock it off (stop simulated combat), checked aircraft systems and we returned to base to debrief. There is no question in my mind that we missed each other by just a few feet if not inches. I truly believe if I had not

◄ **BY THE GRACE OF GOD**

had the intuition that something was not right, I would not be here today. There will be more on intuition later in the book but now is the time to discuss an interesting coincidence that happened early in my life and again much later.

CHAPTER **8**

# Coincidence

I WAS BORN in Greensburg, Indiana in 1944 and my parents lived in a two story home in a town of about 5,000 people. After my birth, my mother and father brought me home from the hospital and placed me in a crib on the second floor of the house and left for a few minutes to do something. A seventeen year old girl lived across the street and she was to be my babysitter. She was downstairs when she heard a strange noise coming from the second floor so she climbed the stairs to see what was happening. When she entered my room, she discovered the back of the house was on fire so she grabbed me, went downstairs, told my parents what was happening and left the house. She, quite probably, saved my life. That's interesting but it's not the whole story.

Fast forward to the year 2002. I was the Mayor of Pensacola and was meeting at the Greater Pensacola Area Chamber of Commerce when I received a call from my assistant at City Hall. She said an elderly couple was asking for me and the lady said she knew me. So I concluded my business with the Chamber drove the three blocks to my office. My assistant had taken the couple to my office and made them comfortable until my arrival. I entered the office and introduced myself and the couple began to explain why they were there. They had been vacationing at Perdido Key and came across a tourism pamphlet that had a letter that I had written to welcome visitors to our area. The lady was now 74 years old and she went on to explain she saw my name on the letter and said to her husband, there can't be that many John Foggs in the world. The 74 year old lady was the 17 year old girl who had saved my life some 57 years earlier. I had heard the story of the fire but I never imagined I would have an opportunity to meet and thank her face to face. A coincidence? Really? Now I would like to introduce you to the 11:11 phenomenon.

CHAPTER 9

# The 11:11 Phenomenon

BEGINNING IN THE 1996 time frame, I began to see 11:11 everywhere and often. At first, I dismissed the experience as coincidence but it kept reoccurring and increased in frequency. At some point, I concluded this could not be coincidence and that statistically, it was not possible in the absence of some sort of spiritual or paranormal reality that was manifesting itself in my world. On several occasions, I awakened from a deep sleep and my digital alarm clock was displaying 11:11. Another notable example of this phenomenon involved the pastor of a local church. I was having a conversation with the pastor in his office and told him about the 11:11 phenomenon and other experiences. We had been talking for about 30 minutes and I noticed a digital clock on his desk that was not displaying the correct time. I asked the pastor about it and he said it had stopped several days ago and so I asked him if he knew the time the clock stopped. He said he didn't know because it was facing away from his chair. I picked up the clock and turned it so he could read the time. The clock had stopped at 11:11. Another example of this experience occurred while

◄ BY THE GRACE OF GOD

attending a lunch meeting of my Rotary Club and guests were being introduced.

One of the guests was a screen writer from New York City who was visiting the area looking for a good location for a motion picture studio. As the Mayor of Pensacola, I introduced myself after the meeting to see if I could help him in his search. We ended up having lunch the next day and in the course of the conversation, he asked me if I was seeing 11:11 everywhere. The rest of our conversation centered on examples of where and how we were both experiencing this phenomenon. Between the two of us, there were hundreds of examples of the manifestation. I did not search the internet for 11:11 at that time but did a few years later. If you search for 1111 or 11:11 or eleven eleven today, you will get 211,000,000 and 366,000,000 and 217,000,000 hits respectively. And if you look at some of the sites, you will find really outrageous interpretations as to what all this might mean. I want to be very clear about this, I ascribe no meaning whatever to the 11:11 phenomenon except this: the 11:11 experience could not have been coincidental. For me, it opened my mind to the reality of a spiritual world I had not before experienced and it was interacting with our material world in such a way it could not have been mere chance. For me, the 11:11 phenomenon began in 1996 and persisted to about 2005 and then it began to wane. This was the first step of my spiritual awakening but I still had no idea what it meant or where it might lead me. The most important result of this experience was that I opened my mind to the existence of a spiritual dimension which is real and present with us as we journey through life in this world. I wrote about the importance of intuition earlier and now I want to tell you about the most important intuition I've ever had.

◄ 60

CHAPTER **10**

# Drawn to the Bible

IN 1997, I felt a very strong need (intuition) to begin reading the Bible. I had read bits and pieces of Scripture over the years but They never really captured my attention. Now things were different. I guess because I had accepted the existence of a spiritual dimension, the Bible came alive for me. As I read certain passages, I realized some of what Jesus described was happening to me. I was a little "put off" by people who claimed they were born again because I had not experienced it.

During one of the Presidential election cycles, a reporter asked George W. Bush if he was born again and he replied that he was. The reporter pressed the President for an explanation of what it meant to be born again. The President responded by asking the reporter if he was born again and the reporter said he wasn't so the President responded by saying "If you haven't experienced it, there is no way to explain it."

I am going to make my best attempt to explain what being born again means to me. As I read more of the Bible, I found myself praying on regular basis and frequently. My prayers were very simple and went something like this. "Father, please send your Holy Spirit upon me and guide me and strengthen me that I would be at the center of Your will for my life." I had reached the point that I knew that surrendering to God's will for my life would be a far better plan than anything I could imagine. As I read and prayed more, I began to perceive a continuum between the purely material and the purely spiritual worlds. Throughout most of my life, I lived in the material world entirely, not being aware of the continuum between the two. The following Scripture really resonated with me: "Ask, and it shall be given you; seek, and ye shall find; knock, and it shall be opened unto you." (Matt 7:7)

As I became more aware of the material/spiritual continuum, I also perceived movement between the material and spiritual as life events unfolded. By now, I was pursuing a personal relationship with the Father through Jesus Christ on a daily basis and I also noticed events of the material world would be a distraction that would tend to draw me back to the material world. Remember, these experiences and my reaction to them was not based on some formula (religion) with the intent of becoming more spiritual. I was being drawn into a personal relationship with God that exceeded anything I thought possible. I have never felt a love as great as this. As I read more about what Jesus was and is about, I began to understand for the first time the depth of God's love for us. He sent His only begotten Son to redeem us, to die on the cross as a perfect sacrifice for our sins, past, present and future. To make the way passable. When I realized that, I felt and understood the conviction of the Holy Spirit. For my part, I wanted to behave in such a way as to

# DRAWN TO THE BIBLE

never add to the burden that Jesus took on Himself on the cross. I believe the Holy Spirit guides us if we will listen and here is an example of that.

I was asked to speak at commencement of our local Junior college. It was a large graduating class with ages varying from 19 to 76. This was a challenging assignment for me and I struggled with what I might say to such a diverse group of people. How could I hold their interest? By this time in my spiritual awakening, I would pray for guidance on a regular basis so I closed the blinds on my office window and closed the door and prayed for inspiration for a meaningful message. What came to me is a powerful concept that can change your life. Most of us define ourselves as the sum of all our life experiences in our past within the context of our relationships with other people. And we look to the future as if it were an entity in and of itself. The concept I want to convey is this: We create the past and the future simultaneously in this moment. With every second that passes, we create our past and with every future activity we schedule, we create our future. But we don't advance into the future, the future recedes into our current moment. Let me explain this another way. Remember the old reel to reel tape recorders? The recorder heads were located between the take up reel and the feeder reel. Sound was recorded on the tape as it was drawn through the heads and then stored on the tape on the take up reel. The take up reel is our past and our history. The feeder reel is essentially blank with exception of the future events that we schedule in this moment. So, as the tape is drawn to the recording heads, those future events get closer to the recording heads or this moment and finally, those future moments recede into our present moment and together, we create the past and the future simultaneously. We cannot change the past once it's done but we do create the future in this moment within the context of our relationships with others and our own actions in this moment. All too often, we define ourselves as the sum of all the events of our past. But in reality, all that really defines us is what we do in this moment. The moment comes and goes in the blink of an eye and it can never be recovered or changed once it is past. If we can fully embrace this concept, every moment we live is invaluable and each one defines our past and future simultaneously

In the PGA world, you hear golfers refer to "being in the moment." The way I interpret that is, they don't allow what happened in the past to interfere with their focus on the moment of their next shot. No matter how bad the last shot was, they are able to put that out of their minds and focus on making the next shot the best ever. The same goes for the future. They don't worry about what the future might bring, they seem to intuitively know if they do their best in this moment, the future will take care of itself.

This same principle applies in the business world without exception. Just imagine what it might look like if we all embraced this concept and acted on it. Then the past becomes a tool from which we learn what worked well in those past moments and what didn't, but we don't let the past define boundaries or expectations. Further, you couple that with the concept that scheduling future events sets the stage for unpopulated future scheduled moments to recede into our current moment to be fully populated in the "now" and then, immediately to become our personal and collective past.

Our capacity to create events and accomplish things in this moment, to a great extent, relies on our relationships with others. But what's even more powerful is a combination of those relationships we have with others and overlay that with our relationship with God and a willingness to be receptive to His guidance through others and the Holy Spirit. I believe God's plan for our lives is a far greater plan than anything we could imagine. It's a matter of being open to His guidance and receptive to His gentle nudging. More on this later but now there are several more experiences I want to relate that point to the spiritual reality manifesting itself in our world.

CHAPTER **11**

# The Viet Nam Experience

THIS CHAPTER IS focused on my experiences in Viet Nam. I arrived "in country" in January of 1970 and in the next 12 months, flew 200 combat air missions out of Chu Lai and Da Nang and served as an advisor to the Korean Marines for a little over three months. I was assigned to VMFA 115, a Marine Fighter/Attack Squadron, with 12 F-4 Phantoms. In general, sixty percent of the missions we flew were close air support of our troops on the ground and the other forty percent were a combination of MIG Combat Air Patrol (enemy aircraft intercept), Barrier Combat Air Patrol (enemy aircraft interdiction), TPQ's (Radar Guided Bombing Missions), Interdiction of supply lines and troop movements and Escort of B-52's, A-6's and A-5's. The Phantom was a very capable and versatile aircraft and every mission was configured with two AIM 7 Sparrow radar guided missiles and two AIM 9 Sidewinder heat seeking missiles. The rest of the ordnance usually included 12 Mark 82 500 pound hard bombs or a mix of 500 pound snake-eyes (retarded) and Napalm. The 500 pound snake-eyes were designed for low altitude release and had fins that would open upon release and retard the bombs behind the aircraft so that, upon detonation, the aircraft would be clear of the frag pattern. Both napalm and snake-eyes were used in close air support with a 10 degree dive angle or less and a release altitude of about 100 feet. The shallow dive angle and low release altitude allowed for a very high level of accuracy and effectiveness. Early in my tour in Viet Nam, my Radar Intercept Officer (RIO) and I were fragged (scheduled) for a single plane interdiction mission and we were loaded with four air to air missiles and 12 Mark 82 500 pound bombs. Our target was a resupply line on the western edge of "I" Corps in northern South Viet Nam and the weather was such that we couldn't use the normal race track pattern in the horizontal to attack and re-attack the target. As a result, we had to execute reversals in the vertical which required the use of the afterburners to maintain energy and airspeed. In full afterburner, the F-4 will burn 600 pounds of JP-5 jet fuel every minute. We had just completed our last bomb run and the minimum fuel light illuminated. That means we had only 2,000 pounds of fuel remaining and that was not enough to get us back to base. If you are an F-4 pilot, you are concerned about fuel constantly, even before takeoff. With a full load of internal fuel of a little over 12,000 pounds, in full afterburner, you can burn it all in less than 20 minutes. The F-4 does have a fuel dump valve which could have malfunctioned but to this day, I cannot understand how we got into this situation but what happened next was nothing short of a miracle. Ejecting from any aircraft in a combat zone is not what you want to do because the North Vietnamese Army (NVA) and the Viet Cong had pretty much free run of most of the country. If you had to eject, you knew you would be in an "escape and evade" scenario and your chances of survival would be in question. So with no other options, I selected UHF Guard frequency of 243.0 megahertz and ask if there were any tankers in the area. The Marine Corps had one KC-130 squadron in country based in Da Nang. To my knowledge, we did not have the assets to keep a tanker airborne all the time but in this case, for whatever the reason, a tanker was airborne and fairly close by. They responded to my call on Guard frequency and we plotted a course to rendezvous. We got a visual on the tanker and they had already deployed the drogue from the left wing refueling pod. We rendezvoused as quickly as possible and extended our refueling probe at the last minute to reduce drag and conserve fuel. At this point, our fuel was down to 600 pounds. The F-4 fuel gage is only accurate to plus or minus 500 pounds so we were really down to fumes. It would be critical to successfully plug into the drogue on the first attempt. If not, we might not get another chance. I stabilized our jet behind the KC-130 just a few feet from the drogue basket and added power just enough to gently close on the basket and then we were in. I checked the fuel gage which confirmed we were taking on fuel and we _all_ could finally breathe again. I am embarrassed to tell this story because we should never have been in this situation in the first place but I feel it is an important example of how God can and does work. If that tanker had been just a few miles further away, I don't think we would have made it. Today, I don't believe it was luck or coincidence. I believe God is at work in our lives all the time if we would just open our hearts and minds to that possibility. There are two other observations about my experience in Viet Nam that I would like to share with you.

## ◂ BY THE GRACE OF GOD

My primary job in Viet Nam was to fly the Phantom on combat air missions. In the Marine Corps, however, you are also assigned other responsibilities and I was designated to be our squadron's ordinance officer. I was working the flight line one afternoon and we got the call. A pilot had been shot down in the Ban Karai Pass on the Ho Chi Minh Trail. The Trail ran from North Viet Nam through Laos and Cambodia then to various entry points into South Viet Nam. It was a route used to move troops and supplies from the north to the south and the Trail was as much as 50 miles wide in some places and 1,000 miles long. There were two mountain passes that were choke points with very little jungle canopy, due to intensive bombing and agent orange, to conceal troop movements. The North Vietnamese knew they had to keep the Trail open if they were going to have any chance of winning the war and we knew we had to interdict that supply line if we intended to win the war. Since the Trail was critical to the North, they deployed an impressive array of anti-aircraft weaponry to the Mu Gia and Ban Karai passes and as a result, any effort to rescue downed aircrew in the passes became a very hazardous endeavor. In this case, several attempts had been made to pick up the pilot but in each case, the helicopters had to retreat because of withering anti-aircraft fire. More and more air assets were brought in to suppress fire and provide cover for the helos but to no avail. The decision was made to lay down a smoke screen so the enemy gunners could not see the helos as they lowered the jungle penetrator to recover the pilot. I was assigned as the flight lead of a two plane sortie to lay down the smoke. Unfortunately, the smoke munitions had very specific limitations on airspeed while dispensing the smoke spheres. In order for the smoke to be most effective,

# THE VIET NAM EXPERIENCE

you had to reduce speed to 250 Kts. for the duration of the deployment. That meant you had to be straight and level for about 12 to 15 seconds and at 250 Kts, while maintaining an altitude of 200' AGL(above ground Level). Further, at 250 Kts, the F-4 only has about 2 G's available so maneuverability would be limited when evasive maneuvers would be required. Long story short, the chances of surviving this mission in this hostile environment were not good. The smoke munitions were loaded on our jets and we suited up and waited for the command to launch. In the meantime, all of our air assets were brought to bear against the anti-aircraft guns. My RIO and I and my wingmen were preparing to man the jets when a call came in from Headquarters. The mission was cancelled. I never did hear what the outcome of the rescue effort was or why the mission was cancelled. I was extremely grateful we didn't have to fly that mission and certainly didn't think about Divine intervention at that point in my life but given everything else I've experienced, you have to wonder.

As I said, the majority of combat missions we flew were close air support, often with allied forces in contact (in combat) with the NVA or Viet Cong. The NVA forces developed a defensive tactic when coming under air attack. As we approached the target, the enemy forces would aim their weapons skyward and open fire in full automatic mode. In other words, they would fill the sky with bullets that we would have to fly though. It is referred to as barrage fire. I remember one mission vividly. We were delivering napalm and 500 Lb. snake eyes and I had just released the ordinance at about 100 feet above ground level, pulled the nose up and broke to the right

◄ **BY THE GRACE OF GOD**

and could see the enemy soldiers with their weapons on full automatic shooting at me. I never thought anything of it at the time, but it is interesting to note that my airplane never took a hit the whole time I was in Viet Nam. Perhaps many other pilots had the same experience...I just think it is worth relating within the context of this book. There is one other aviation based experience I want to relate that you might find interesting.

CHAPTER **12**

# The Gear Up Landing

I RETURNED TO the United States in January of 1971 and had requested assignment to the Naval Air Training Command in Pensacola as a flight instructor. In order to even be considered for assignment to the Blue Angels, you must have a minimum of 1500 flight hours in a tactical jet. There is no better way to build flight time than in the training command. You have the latitude to conduct training missions on the weekends which fit well with the requirement to join the Blues at airshow sites as part of the application process. The Blues were flying shows in the northeast that weekend which would require a refueling stop at NAS Oceana. I was assigned to a training squadron flying the T-2C Buckeye. The T-2C was a very capable twin engine jet used for intermediate jet training which included carrier landing qualification, air to air gunnery and other qualifications to prepare student naval aviators for the fleet. My student and I departed NAS Pensacola on Friday morning with a refueling stop planned at Oceana. It was a beautiful day and weather was not a factor and the flight was uneventful until our arrival at the air station. The tower cleared us for the break so we lined up with

## BY THE GRACE OF GOD

the duty runway, accelerated to over 400 KTS at an altitude of 1,000' above ground level (AGL). In Naval Aviation, the break is flown as if you're preparing to land on an aircraft carrier. At sea, the break is flown at 600' above mean sea level (MSL) and you commence a hard left turn, pulling 6 G's or so at the round down or stern of the boat, reduce power to idle and extend the speed breaks. As soon as you decelerate to gear speed, you extend the gear and flaps and continue to bleed energy until you slow to "on speed" angle of attack. The only difference between the land and at sea break is the initial altitude which is 1,000' over land. To this point, everything was normal and going as planned. We broke at the numbers with a hard left turn and began to slow down. As soon as we decelerated to gear speed, we knew we had a problem. I attempted to place the gear handle in the down position and I felt resistance to the movement of the handle and could not place the handle in the proper position to begin the extension of the landing gear. We notified the tower, declared an emergency and began the execution of the emergency procedures for this situation. We performed a low pass by the tower so they could perform a visual inspection of the gear and they confirmed that none of our wheels were down. One situation we could not tolerate is the chance one of the main landing gear would partially or fully extend which would create an asymmetrical condition that would be dangerous upon contact with the runway. To reduce that chance, I had my student pilot forcibly hold the gear handle in the gear up position while we maneuvered for a gear up landing. Normally, when landing gear up on a runway, the operations and crash, fire and rescue (CFR) people would spray a fire retardant foam on the runway to minimize the chance of fire upon contact with the

## THE GEAR UP LANDING

runway. In this case however, we had insufficient fuel remaining to complete the foaming process. We informed tower of our fuel state and advised them we had to put the airplane on the ground soon. Tower cleared us to land and deployed the crash, fire and rescue vehicles and crews to respond in the event of a fire on touchdown. Normally, Navy and Marine Corps fixed wing aircraft fly an approach glide slope that results in 700 feet per minute rate of descent all the way to touch down and the landing gear are designed for that kind of impact while landing on an aircraft carrier. In this case, you strive to reduce the rate of descent to near zero at touch down to minimize damage to the aircraft and injury to the crew. This particular runway was equipped with centerline lighting so it was necessary to offset from centerline to prevent further damage to the aircraft and to the centerline lighting system. I flew the jet to a few feet above the runway and inched our way down to contact with the ground. As soon as I felt the airplane touch down, I shut the engines down to reduce foreign object damage (FOD) to the engines and eased the stick forward slightly to kill any lift and increase the friction between the aircraft and the ground to slow us down a little faster. It didn't take long for the airplane to come to a complete stop and the crash, fire and rescue people quickly surrounded us and foamed the crash site to knock down a small fire under the aircraft. The last thing for us to do was egress the aircraft in case of an uncontrolled fire. I secured the master power switch which allowed us to raise the canopy with no weight on the wheels and we jumped over the side. Once out of the jet, I do remember giving into my anger that the airplane had a system failure and I derived some satisfaction by kicking the side of the jet. Aircrews are trained for these

## BY THE GRACE OF GOD

kinds of emergencies but none the less, a gear up landing with no foam in a jet aircraft can be dicey. I didn't think anything of it at the time. After all, aircrews are expected to handle these things. But, given my new perspective, I believe God was in the middle of this also. There are two more experiences I want to relate and then we'll move on to what this spiritual awakening has meant to me.

CHAPTER 13

# The Ruptured Natural Gas Line

WE WERE STATIONED in Beaufort, South Carolina and Pat and I were driving to downtown Beaufort and we were stopped at a red light. There was construction work underway and a backhoe was just a few feet away from us. The operator was digging a trench parallel to the road and I could tell the machine had caught on something. The operator continued to apply more pressure and the backhoe broke free and a geyser of dirt and gas erupted just a few feet from us. He had ruptured the main gas line for the entire city. If you search the internet for gas line explosions, you will find they are quite common and often deadly. At the time, I thought we were just lucky that it didn't explode. Today, I don't think luck had anything to do with it. I believe God is present in our lives all the time. That's even if we don't believe we have been born again or claim to be Christian. Let's move on to another experience that had a life changing effect on me.

CHAPTER 14

# Divine Intervention

PENSACOLA, FOUNDED IN 1559 by Don Tristan DeLuna, is the first European settlement in what is now the United States. Since its founding, five national flags have flown over our city and they are the Spanish, French, English, Confederate and American. Every year, we celebrate our heritage with the Fiesta of Five Flags which is the oldest celebration of its kind in Florida. Many events are scheduled over a ten day period and one of my favorites is the Fiesta Boat Parade. About 30 boats form up at the Pensacola Yacht Club to transport Don Tristan DeLuna and his Court to Pensacola Beach to reenact his landing and settlement of the Pensacola Bay area. I was Mayor at the time and my job was to present a proclamation from the City to DeLuna and his Court to commemorate the occasion. Pat and I along with several other community leaders were on a 68 foot motor yacht and we tied up to the dock starboard side to. The deck of the boat was about five feet above the dock so the crew mounted a gangway on the starboard side for people to get on and off the boat. The steps and handrail were attached to the boat with stainless steel clevis pins that locked into permanently mounted brackets on the deck. For a clevis pin to be installed or removed, a button must be depressed and held. At the bottom of the steps were two castors that rested on the dock. As the boat moved relative to the dock, the castors would allow the gangway to move freely. We had been at the dock for about 45 minutes and it was time to leave the boat and go ashore to welcome DeLuna and his Court and present the proclamation. Many people had gone up and down the gangway before it was time for Pat and me to go ashore. I had a drink in one hand and the proclamation in the other and stepped on the top step of the gangway. That placed my feet about five feet above the dock and over the water between the boat's hull and the dock. I remember seeing the bottom steps of the gangway start to shift to the left and all of the sudden, I couldn't hear anything, even though a band was playing and hundreds of people were in close proximity splashing in the water and otherwise having a good time. Concurrent with my loss of hearing, it was as if my eyes were about 18 inches above what looked like one of the boards on the dock and the grain of the wood was very apparent. All of the sudden, my sight and hearing were restored and I was standing flat footed on the dock. I was standing between the steps of the gangway and the handrail which had struck my right thigh with enough force to leave a bruise. Even more remarkably, I didn't fall down or spill my drink or drop the proclamation. The yacht's crew inspected the gangway and discovered the starboard clevis pin had somehow backed out of the bracket mounted on the deck which allowed the gangway to fall down and to the left. Clevis pins lock into place and backing out of a mounting bracket is not supposed to be possible. In addition to that, somehow, I had moved two feet laterally and five feet vertically and landed on my feet with no recollection of how it happened. There is a humorous sidebar to this story also. A friend of mine, who happens to be an attorney, witnessed the event and he came to my side, put his arm around me and asked, "When do you want to take delivery of this yacht." Upon hearing that, another attorney was on the fly bridge who had also seen it happen said, "Take your hands off my client." Apparently, they believed the event was serious enough to warrant their joking about a law suit. Pat and I went on to present the proclamation and after returning to the yacht, I sat down with the captain of the boat who had also seen the gangway failure. He was concerned that I might have been injured and wanted to be sure I was OK. I told him I was fine and that I was very lucky. He looked me square in the eyes and said, "Luck had nothing to do with it" without explaining what he meant by that. I thought it then and still believe it now, that this experience is a clear example of Divine intervention. The loss of sight and hearing is profound. For me, it is proof positive that God certainly exists and that He and/or other spiritual beings are engaged with us in some way every day. The next thing I want to share with you is the most difficult experience of my life but it needs to be told.

CHAPTER **15**

# How Did This Happen?

BY THE YEAR 1997, I was no longer unsure about the experience I was having. Clearly, I was being drawn to the Bible and it was becoming more meaningful to me with every passing day. Pat and I are as close as two people can be, we enjoy doing everything together. We met each other racing sailboats and discovered we both have a great love of boating and sailing. We owned several sailboats over the years and have never tired of being on the water and we both loved the competition of yacht racing. Pat was not an accomplished watercolorist when we married so I had the privilege of watching her grow in her skill. She studied under some of the best artists in the country including an internationally recognized master Chinese watercolorist. Pat picked up that technique with ease and before long, she rivaled her teacher in her quality of work. Pat started competing in regional art festivals and soon she was recognized and the recipient of many awards. Further, Pat possesses a deep well of creativity which she demonstrates on a daily basis. She mastered the techniques of Chinese watercolors and decided she wanted to do something new and without any coaching, she painted an original in the American Watercolor Tradition. Her first painting in that style received a second in show at the Beaufort Water Festival. Based on her love of the water and nature, Pat painted several original watercolors on NOAA Nautical Charts which she then had printed. Over the years, she has sold thousands of the prints in Pensacola, Mobile, New Orleans, Orange Beach, Destin, Hilton Head Island and Savannah.

I could go on and on but the point is that Pat is incredibly talented and I very much enjoyed being part of her growth as an artist. Today, she is still growing and introduces new media regularly.

In 2001, I was retained as a Marketing Consultant with a Florida based tissue bank and a month after that, Pat was hired as a regional director. That meant Pat and I could help the company but in different capacities and we did that for eleven years. The point is that once again, we had the opportunity to work and play together in everything we did and we enjoyed every minute of it.

Early in the book, I mentioned my involvement in politics with the City of Pensacola. Pat and I did that for over 20 years and it is important for me to acknowledge that. Any of you who have held elected office know what I mean. Being in politics is not like going to work every day and coming home that evening while leaving the work at the office. It is an hour by hour commitment that both husband and wife make in service to the community. There is no way to compartmentalize your work as an elected official or put it aside for discussion later. At least for

## HOW DID THIS HAPPEN?

us, if there was an unresolved issue out there, that's what we talked about in our "down time." All this points to the assertion I made earlier…that we enjoy doing everything together and that we love each other on top of that. Before we move on, I want to tell you about Pat's and my religious background.

Pat grew up in Pensacola and she and her parents had long been Episcopalians. Pat and her parents are charter members of the church and were deeply involved in most of the church programs throughout their lives. I became an Episcopalian when Pat and I were married. Pat and I both have served on the Vestry of the church and Pat has served in many capacities including President of the Episcopal Church Women (ECW) and as Chairman of their annual fund raiser for local charities. My background is a little different. I grew up in Greensburg, Indiana and my father was Catholic and my mother was Baptist. My mother didn't attend the Baptist church but attended the Catholic Church with me, my father and my two older brothers. My father was a very devout Catholic and we attended church every Sunday. My father was a hardware salesman with a five state region to cover, so he was on the road during the week most of the time but when he was home during the week, it was our tradition to say the rosary together on Wednesday evenings. My dad would gather us in a room and turn off the lights and we would say the rosary together three times. I was eight or nine at the time and I really didn't understand the significance of what we were doing. My mother was a licensed teacher in Indiana and my grandfather had been the Superintendent of Schools in Decatur County. We only had one parochial school in Greensburg and when my oldest brother became school aged, my parents decided to send us all to the public school, believing the quality of education at the parochial school was substandard. My parents' decision was challenged by the local Catholic priest but they would not change their minds. As a result, the priest began excommunication proceedings against my father. The proceedings went all the way to the Vatican. If you know anything about the Catholic religion, you know excommunication is the most serious action the church can take against a member. My father was devastated but he would not back down. The Vatican eventually dismissed the request by the priest but he would not relent. The priest unilaterally prohibited my father from taking communion in his church, the only Catholic Church in Greensburg. Again, my father was devastated. He began to have some medical problems and on July 4th, 1955, at the age of 45, he committed suicide. I was 10 years old. Shortly after that, a new priest had come to the church. He was a young man and we were talking after Mass one Sunday. He knew my background and I asked him about my father's death, hoping for some spiritual insight or some comforting thought. The new priest's comment was this: "Sometimes life is a bucket of shit." Are you kidding?! That day, I ceased to be a Catholic. I don't blame the Church for these events but I do believe the priest that brought these actions against my father contributed to his death.

I finished public school in Greensburg in 1963 and went on to Butler University in Indianapolis where I graduated with a degree in psychology in 1967. I think I chose psychology hoping that I might have a better understanding of my father's death. From the time I was 10 years old up until my 55th birthday, I still

## HOW DID THIS HAPPEN?

considered myself to be a Christian but I wasn't a consistent member of any church. With this background, my spiritual rebirth could not have been predicted or anticipated in any way.

As my spiritual awakening unfolded, and as my spiritual understanding and my love for Jesus grew, for whatever reason, I totally failed to share with Pat what was happening. Instead of my becoming more loving, it appeared to her and me that I was drifting away. I spoke earlier about compartmentalization as a good thing for a combat pilot. In this case, I believe I used that ability where it was inappropriate. I put our marriage in one box and my spiritual awakening in another. And I was doing some things that I never did before. I started spending time on the internet trying to find other people that were having the same experience as I was, and I did, but I didn't tell Pat about those contacts. It was deceitful. All of this was out of character for me. Pat and I had always shared in everything but I began to think I could not continue to grow spiritually in our marriage. I thought I had to choose between my relationship with Pat and my relationship with God. **I was wrong about that** but those were my thoughts at the time. So, I moved out of our house in July of 1999 and rented an apartment. As a matter of fact, when I finished moving into my apartment that evening, I remember saying, almost shouting, "How the hell did this happen!!!" To put my feelings in context, you have to understand what it was like for Pat and me when the Marine Corps gave me orders to an unaccompanied tour overseas or to an aircraft carrier. Being separated from Pat was as if she had died. The separation was unbearable for me. Yet, in this situation, I inflicted that same sense of loss on both of us willfully. It was irrational. As

## BY THE GRACE OF GOD

I write now of my actions then, I am ashamed of the way I left Pat, without any conversation and without regard for the deep emotional wound I was inflicting. She did nothing to deserve that and I wish I could rewrite history but I can't. I wish I had gone to counseling before I moved out so that I could better understand what was happening to me. If I had, we could have avoided all of this. I will regret not making the decision to go to counseling for the rest of my life. God does not call you and expect or demand that your marriage be damaged. For those of you having a similar experience as mine, please find a way to not make the mistakes I did. Pat and I were separated for about seven months and towards the end of that period, we did go to counseling and I realized how irrational my actions had been. After I finally understood my spiritual awakening and put it in the proper context, our marriage was strengthened and our love is stronger than ever. And finally, I need to thank Pat for having the faith and hope that I would return to the person she knew and loved but with a strong spiritual foundation. I didn't deserve the patience she exhibited and I wish I could take back the hurt I caused her. She is a "saint" and I love her more every day and "By the Grace of God," our marriage survived.

CHAPTER **16**

# The Awakening

I HOPE YOU have found the experiences I have related to be interesting and helpful to you. When you consider the totality of those events, at least for me, it points to the existence of a spiritual reality that is interacting with all of us every day, whether we know it or not. There are many more experiences I could relate that would serve to reinforce my belief that the God of the New Testament exists and that He is active in our lives all the time. What I would like to do now is address some of the teachings in the new testament that are much more meaningful to me now than they ever were before my spiritual awakening. The Scriptures quoted here are from the King James Version of the Bible because it is considered in the public domain. I would encourage you to cross reference these passages with the NIV or other newer translations of the Bible. I was always a little "put off" by people who claimed to be born again because I hadn't experienced it. We talked a little earlier about Jesus' assertion, "Verily, verily, I say unto thee, Except a man be born again, he cannot see the kingdom of God." (John 3:3). He was speaking to Nicodemus, a member of the Jewish ruling council.

### BY THE GRACE OF GOD

Nicodemus didn't understand what Jesus meant so Jesus went on to say "Verily, verily, I say unto thee, Except a man be born of water and of the Spirit, he cannot enter into the kingdom of God. That which is born of the flesh is flesh; and that which is born of the Spirit is spirit." (John 3:5-6). Earlier in the book I spoke of a continuum between the material world and the spiritual world. The more I prayed, the more aware I became of the guidance and conviction of the Holy Spirit. For me, being born again is the realization of the continuum between the material and spiritual and where I am on it. As I focus on the Lord, I feel closer to Him and more receptive to the guidance of the Holy Spirit. And my love and appreciation for Jesus grows stronger. Jesus also said "No man can come to me, except the Father which hath sent me draw him." (John 6:44). That's exactly what happened to me. As I said earlier, I was not seeking anything spiritual. I was happy with my circumstance and I didn't feel like anything was missing in my life. It began subtly with a desire to play Mannheim Steamroller Christmas music on the way to and from work in the middle of the summer. Ultimately, I was led to read the Bible and as I said earlier, it came alive for me and led to a personal relationship with God that the Bible promises. Let's talk about that.

Jesus said "For God so loved the world that he gave his only begotten Son, that whosoever believeth in him should not perish, but have everlasting life." (John 3:16) For me, the key words here are love and everlasting. God wants us to have a relationship with Him and through Jesus Christ, we can. Even more than that, Jesus took upon himself the burden of our sins by His death on the cross and by His resurrection, He overcame the

# THE AWAKENING

world and death and made the way passable for us to be children of God and to have eternal life through our belief in Jesus Christ. Jesus was the perfect sacrifice for our sins, past, present and future so that we can enter into the presence of God, having been cleansed of our sins. For me, a sin is any thought, action, deed or omission that interferes with or diminishes our relationship with God. At the core of this relationship is love which flows both ways. I believe hell is a place where souls go after death where they are totally separated from God's love for eternity. I want to tell you about an experience I had while all this was unfolding in my life. I am a little reluctant to include this experience for some will say this is not possible or think I have lost my mind. Nevertheless, it is important in our discussion of God's love for us. I was the Mayor of Pensacola at the time and I had just arrived at my office at City Hall. By this time, my relationship with God and Jesus had become very real and beautiful. Almost every day was like Christmas as I became more aware of God's presence in my life. At some point in the afternoon, my thoughts turned to God and I was overwhelmed by a feeling of love so intense that my rational mind could not process it. I was debilitated to the point I could not speak and I felt a joy so intense that there are no words to express the gratitude and unworthiness I felt. In a few minutes, the feelings began to dissipate and things got back to normal, except that I will remember and cherish the experience for the rest of my life.

I am told some people resist embracing Christianity because they don't want to do, or not do, the things they perceive as life style changes that would be required. The apostle Paul had this to say: "Therefore if any man be in Christ, he is a new creature:

## BY THE GRACE OF GOD

old things are passed away; behold, all things are become new." (2 Corinthians 5:17) In my experience, this is the way it works. When you ask Christ into your life, several things happen. First, the Holy Spirit takes up residence in you and you become more spiritually aware. As this happens, you see Christ as the example and you begin to seek God's will in your life and you begin to change. Not because you have to but because you want to. The Holy Spirit will give you the strength to become the person, and the spirit, that God gave you the potential to be. The apostle Paul had this to say about the Spirit: "But the fruit of the Spirit is love, joy, peace, longsuffering, gentleness, goodness, faith, meekness, temperance: against such there is no law." (Galatians 5:22-23) I believe, that no matter what your circumstance, through the Spirit, you can experience the fruit of the Spirit. When you exhibit those characteristics, I believe people notice it. I was on the seventh floor of city hall one day talking with our receptionist. I noticed the Chief of Police had just met with the City Attorney and was approaching us and the elevators. Please understand, this Chief was the stereotypical police officer with a stern demeanor and appearance. If you are a bad guy, you don't want to commit a crime and have this Chief come after you. As the Chief approached, I greeted him and his response was "I don't know what it is you've got, but I want some of it." Today, I believe I know what it was that he was perceiving. I think it was the fruit of the Spirit. Before we move on from the Holy Spirit, let's talk about the conviction of the Holy Spirit.

After I had asked Christ to come into my heart, I began to change and feel the conviction of the Holy Spirit. Sometimes, it is a small correction where I wished I hadn't said something the way I did. Sometimes I am moved to apologize for something I said or some action I took. Sometimes, the Spirit reinforces the good things you do. A larger example is this book. God has given me an incredible gift and if I were to die without sharing this experience with others, in my mind and spirit, it would be a terrible tragedy. The Holy Spirit convicted me of that.

If I were to sum up the message of this book, it is that you are loved and you are more valuable than you may know. This book is a message of hope, no matter what your circumstance, that you too, can go through this life while enjoying the fruits of the Spirit. My prayer is that you will feel the love and peace that only Christ can provide. No matter what your situation, rich or poor, healthy or not, if you feel something is missing in your life, a simple prayer can fill the void. It goes something like this: "Father, I am sorry for the things that I have done or left undone that have hindered my relationship with You. Please forgive me. You have promised that if I open my heart, Jesus will be with me now and forever. Today, my heart is open and I pray that you would send Your Holy Spirit upon me to guide me and help me to be at the center of Your will for my life. I ask this in the name of your Son and my Savior, Jesus Christ. Amen."

If you just said that prayer with conviction from your heart, your life will be changed forever. You have the capacity to love and be loved beyond comprehension. It is my greatest hope and prayer that you and your eternal soul will come to know the joy of being in Christ.

### BY THE GRACE OF GOD

I want to leave you with this last quote from Scripture: "The Lord is not slack concerning his promise, as some men count slackness; but is longsuffering to us-ward, not willing that any should perish, but should come to repentance." (2 Peter 3:9) There is nothing I can say to convince you God is real. Nor would I try. That decision is between you and God. Most importantly, God does not exclude anyone. Every one of us is important to Him. For me, my trust in God is no longer a matter of faith. It is a matter of "knowing." It is my prayer that you would experience the peace that only a personal relationship with God through Jesus Christ can provide. May God bless you always!

# About the Author

JOHN FOGG WAS raised in Greensburg, Indiana and received a Bachelor of Arts degree from Butler University in Indianapolis, Indiana in 1967. He completed a distinguished 20 year career in the United States Marine Corps as a fighter pilot and retired in 1987 as a Lieutenant Colonel. He flew 200 combat air missions in Viet Nam, earning 14 Air Medals with Combat V. He also served as Air Liaison Officer to the Korean Marines on the ground in South Viet Nam's "I" Corps. He was selected to serve as the Marine Corps Representative with the Navy's Flight Demonstration Squadron, "The Blue Angels." Lieutenant Colonel Fogg is a graduate of the Navy's Fighter Weapons School, "Top Gun" and is a former Commanding Officer of VMFA 122, a Marine Corps fighter squadron. Upon retirement from the Corps, he was awarded the Meritorious Service Medal.

Mr. Fogg and his wife Pat moved to Pensacola, Florida in 1987 where he completed a Master of Public Administration degree from Troy University and embarked on a career in marketing and public relations. Concurrently, he was elected to the Pensacola City Council in 1989 and two subsequent terms.

### BY THE GRACE OF GOD

He was appointed Mayor in July of 1994 and would serve in that capacity for over 14 years, longer than any previous Mayor in Pensacola's history and in 2001, he became the first elected Mayor since 1913. He was designated Mayor Emeritus of Pensacola in January 2009 and served in the Pensacola City government for over 20 years. Mayor Fogg is a sought after motivational speaker who has traveled extensively in that capacity. He is a Past Commodore of Pensacola Yacht Club and he and his wife Pat love boating and other related activities and they will celebrate their 40th anniversary in 2014.